Old House Plans

Also by the Author

The Old House Catalogue
Waiting for the 5:05: Terminal, Station, and Depot in America

Lawrence Grow

Old House Plans

Two Centuries of American Domestic Architecture

A Main Street Press Book

Universe Books   New York

Library of Congress Catalog Card Number 77-91927

ISBN 0-87663-981-3

Published by Universe Books
381 Park Avenue South
New York City 10016

Produced by The Main Street Press
42 Main Street
Clinton, New Jersey 08809

Printed in the United States of America

Cover design by Robert Reed

Contents

Preface

Architectural history is the story of styles, materials, and methods. It is of necessity approached in a case-by-case fashion. Just as the student of law studies the great arguments of the past and the decisions reached by eminent jurists, the formal study of architecture requires a knowledge of what constitutes the best in building design and how this was achieved. Little attention is paid to the failures or even the commonplace. The vast majority of the old houses in which people live today, nevertheless, are of the commonplace sort. One hundred years ago they might even have been considered failures. They are vernacular renderings of classically defined styles. The history of great houses and their master designers has been written many times; the vernacular dwelling, often the work of a carpenter-builder, is rarely studied or explained. With the growth of an historical preservation movement which encompasses much more than the masterpieces or the historically-important George-Washington-Slept-Here kind of house, information on what was done on the everyday level is badly needed. Almost any building which has managed to survive the mad pursuit of material progress in North America is surely deserving of such study. *Old House Plans* seeks to meet that need.

Various builders' handbooks and compilations of designs have been reprinted in recent years. These are of inestimable value in documenting the history of a popular style and may even provide specific details which aid those seeking to restore or otherwise preserve a period building. Circulation of these reprints, however, has been limited to a fairly small circle of enthusiasts. They are the first to agree that the time has arrived to disseminate this material in more popular form.

Old House Plans covers thirteen building styles popular in North America from the seventeenth to the early years of the twentieth century. Elevations, floor plans, perspectives, and detail drawings of individual homes—most of which have been taken from period sources—are given as illustrations of the development and use of specific architectural forms and elements. Where interior arrangements are known, these are specified. None of the examples can be considered typical in every respect. The "average" house does not exist. But there is enough which is stylistically common about the examples to offer them as guidelines. Hopefully, the reader, once attracted to these keys to architectural scripture, will seek to dig much further for the roots of the old house of his liking.

The Colonial Style

"Colonial," like "Victorian," is a stylistic term which defies precise definition. The Colonial aesthetic as practiced by pre-Revolutionary carpenters, builders, and architects varied widely from colony to colony and even within the provincial boundaries of the time. At least five distinct "Colonial" styles have been recognized by historians—Spanish, New England, Southern, French, and Dutch. Domestic Colonial architecture in America was of a vernacular sort; to what extent the practitioners of the style followed a dictated sense of princples is nearly impossible to determine in most of their buildings. After the mid-eighteenth century, it is clear that there was some reliance on the rule and pattern books of England and American carpenters and architects, but the design and construction of all but the most expensive of homes were at best informal undertakings.

Each generation of Americans since the Revolution has considered the Colonial style in terms of a particular time and place. To small-time farmers or craftsmen building new homes in sparsely populated areas during the first half of the nineteenth century, the Colonial form was the one they knew and held on to as traditional. It was also affordable. Little thought could be given by them to more fashionable developments in architecture. To the newly-rich merchants of East Coast cities in the 1820s and '30s, Colonial was a primitive, "old-fashioned" form best left to the past and replaced with the more decorative and classical forms of the Greek or Gothic Revivals. By the time of the Centennial, however, Americans of the middle and upper classes were beginning to indulge a nostalgia for their Colonial past. The "New England Log House" displayed at the International Exhibition in Philadelphia was celebrated along with the patriotic feats of Revolutionary ancestors. A swing away from the Victorian Gothic and Queen Anne styles was clearly evident by the 1890s. Loose interpretations of seventeenth- and eighteenth-century forms—including the Spanish, New England, and Southern Colonial—constituted what is now known as the "Colonial Revival," and this trend has continued in vernacular as architecture to the present. Architectural fashion, at least in profile, had come full circle.

Throughout the seventeenth and eighteenth centuries the Colonial style was in a state of constant development. Firmly rooted in medieval building practices, it reached its most sophisticated expression in the greater use of brick, elaborate wood millwork, and expanded dimensions during the Georgian period of the mid- to late-eighteenth century.

Although it is impossible to designate as the ultimate word in "Colonial" the building forms of seventeenth- and eighteenth-century Virginia, or New Jersey, or Connecticut (much less the ersatz reproductions of these in knotty-pine twentieth-century style), it is possible to decipher certain characteristics which remained relatively constant over a long period of time from the establishment of the first frontier on the East Coast to the last in the West. We are, of course, dealing here with generalizations; anyone seeking to restore a Colonial dwelling must refer to specifics of a given time and area.

The first dwellings were unadorned and structurally simple. Those that remain today are praised for their directness, their honesty. Most setlers built only what they could afford with materials readily at hand and in a style with which they were already familiar. This meant in most cases a dwelling of one and a half or two stories which was probably only one-room deep. The first "center-hall" Colonials contained two rooms on the principal floor, one of which served as a kitchen and the other as a parlor. In New England, one chimney of stone and plaster rose in the center of the house and usually contained two fireplaces, one for each of the two principal rooms. In the South and in areas settled by the Dutch in the Middle Atlantic states, the fireplaces were usually placed on the gable ends of the house. The second floor, if more than an attic, provided sleeping as well as storage space. It was common practice, however, for beds to be set up on the first floor. Both parlor and kitchen, sometimes termed the "hall," were true family rooms of the time. Many houses contained a cellar which was at least half the size of the house.

The majority of the homes were of wood, some of stone, and a few of brick, that material being a much more expensive medium in which to build. The familiar image of a clapboard structure is not a twentieth-century invention; the exterior walls of many early houses were covered in this manner. Clapboards, usually of oak until late in the Colonial period when pine came into use, were an improvement on the weather boards of a wider width which had been used earlier in England and on the Continent to protect plastered walls. Oak and pine were also employed in the interior in the form of wainscoting and completely paneled walls. Paint was rarely used; plaster walls were merely whitewashed. Glass came into currency slowly, and at first could be afforded only by the wealthy. Window openings, small by necessity, were closed up by the use of wooden shutters or in combination with cloth or oiled paper. Double sashes were a mid-eighteenth century improvement; casement windows were the early norm.

The first weather-beaten Colonials were, then, extremely primitive structures; they can be called picturesque today. They bear little resemblance—except in their box-like profile—to the comfortably furnished and well-tended dwellings featured in *Yankee, Antiques,* or *Southern Living.* Colonial-style dwellings which have not been "improved" in some way, however, are difficult to find. While closet stairs or tightwinders and oppressively low ceilings may remain in many small dwellings, the majority of such homes were altered during the Colonial period and, of course, later. The most common addition to the basic two-room dwelling was the lean-to on the back or the addition of an el. At the same time these changes were being made, entirely new houses, two rooms deep, were being built. These larger Colonial dwellings were much more likely to incorporate the use of glass and more elaborate woodwork. The only impediment to the expansion and elaboration of the basic dwelling at the time, as today, was hard cash.

The Benjamin House in Milford, Connecticut (as sketched in 1900), is representative of a modest eighteenth-century New England Colonial dwelling built in an improved manner as late as the 1760s. It boasts eight and a half foot ceilings, double sash windows, fireplaces on the first and second floors, and a kitchen lean-to. A cooking fireplace and oven are included in the kitchen section and are incorporated in the central chimney of stone. Beams in the first floor rooms have been plastered over. Such structural elements were increasingly hidden from view as the average home owner had little of the modern's appreciation for the rustic. The presence of a fireplace on the second floor indicates that the space was being used more formally for bedrooms, in this case as many as three or four. The stairway is a much more ample, navigable passageway to the upper floors than a tightwinder would have been.

The Ebenezer Grant House in East Windsor, Connecticut, displays fully-developed Colonial-Georgian form, a four-room center-hall structure with an el "servicing wing," chimneys set to each side and built of brick above the roof line, straightforward stairways with convenient landings, and handsomely detailed doorways. Note, however, that one of

the principal first-floor rooms still serves as a bedroom. Beams in most areas of the house were completely plastered over, and walls in the kitchen and in more formal front areas of the house contain expanses of fine paneling.

Benjamin House, Milford, Connecticut

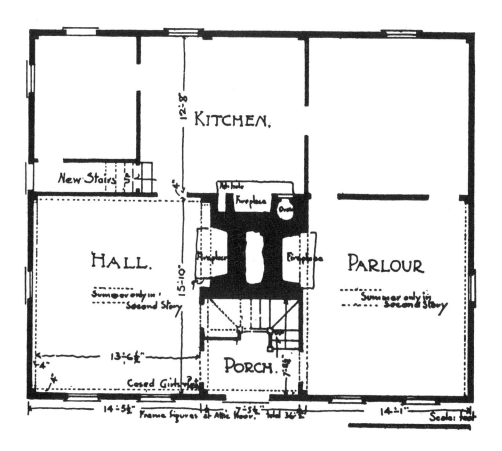

First story, Benjamin House

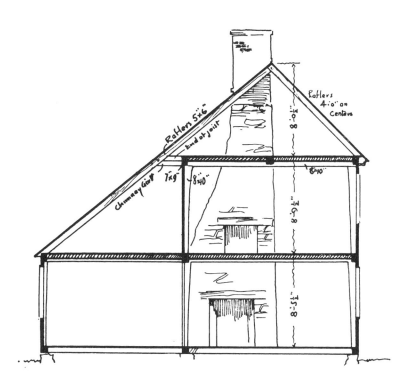

Section, Benjamin House

Ebenezer Grant House, East Windsor, Connecticut

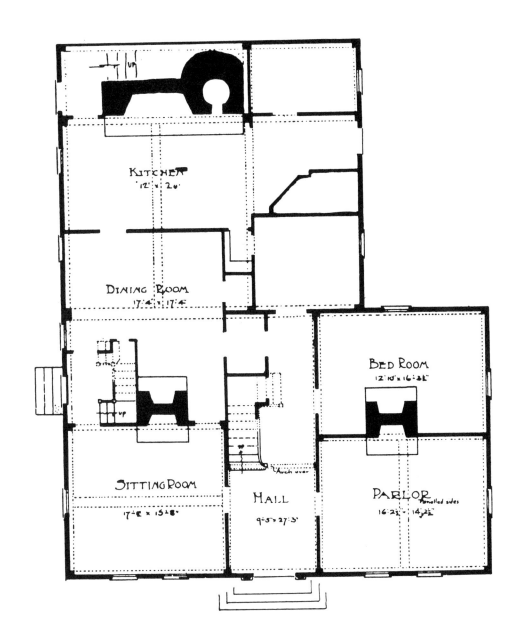

KITCHEN
12' x 20'

DINING ROOM
17'4" x 17'4"

SITTING ROOM
17'6" x 15'8"

HALL
9'5" x 27'3"

BED ROOM
12'10" x 16'3½"

PARLOR
Panelled sides
16'2½" x 14'2½"

Arch over

up

First story, Grant House

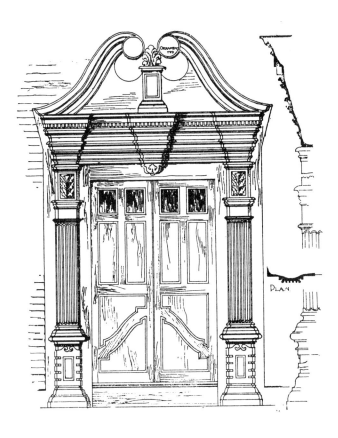

PLAN.

Front entrance, Grant House

The Federal Style

No more felicitous architectural style than the Federal can be encountered in North America. Neoclassical in form and spirit and derivative of the work of the English Adam brothers, particularly Robert, the Federal or Adamesque style became a fashionable mode of building in the 1780s, and its popularity continued until at least the 1820s. Charles Bulfinch of Boston is generally credited with having introduced the style to the United States in 1787. As with other "revivals" of the eighteenth and nineteenth centuries, the passion for neoclassical forms in decoration and building arrived in America after they had been widely popularized in England. The progression from Georgian Palladian forms to the more chaste Adamesque was a natural one in the mercantile capitals of England. In America, where a war of independence led by a merchant class seeking political *and* economic freedom, the spirit of the ancient republics were particularly welcomed. And in the hands of American architects and carpenter-builders from Maine to Georgia, the clean, stoic lines of classical inspiration replaced those of the more opulent, convoluted Georgian. The Federal may be considered America's first national style. It complements architecturally the decorative motifs and schemes adopted for coinage, emblems, and seals, and parallels the taste for a simple classical elegance in furniture and clothing termed "Empire."

The "Federal," an American stylistic term reflective of the new republic, was a particularly appropriate one for public buldings—state houses, churches, custom houses, and other national governmental office buildings. Bulfinch selected it for the Massachusetts State House, and architects elsewhere—amateur or otherwise—followed his example. It was not long before home owners in small and large cities began building along neoclassical lines. Structures in what were then considered heavily populated areas—Boston, New York, Providence, Philadelphia—and in the South were generally built of brick. In Northern cities, disastrous fires in the eighteenth century had prompted the adoption of codes which prohibited the erection of wood structures. But in more rural areas of New England and of the Middle Atlantic states, the Federal style was often interpreted in wood. Perhaps nowhere is this more evident than in Salem, Massachusetts, where master woodcarver and architect Samuel McIntire created a virtual community of handsomely formed and embellished homes for the town's merchant class.

The bow-front town houses of Boston are the most obvious visual reminders of the Federal period in architecture. Although most houses in the style were squarish structures with little or no break in line, there was an attempt to relate external dimensions and internal spatial considerations. The use of bow-fronts, Venetian entrances with fan- and sidelights, and window recesses formed by semicircular relieving arches, are all evidence of an aesthetic consideration for light and geometric form. Room heights, of course, were much greater than that found in the typical Colonial of an earlier period. Windows, however, were generally of narrower dimensions than those found in Georgian buildings. Roofs were pitched at a lower angle and were not corniced as elaborately. On wooden structures, the boards were of a narrower variety than Colonial clapboard; on brick structures, a fine English bond rather than the Flemish was favored for many Georgian-style homes.

The Federal was the first of the American styles to be given popular attention through the printed word. This took the form of handbooks or builder's guides, the most famous of which was Asher Benjamin's *The American Builder's Companion*, first published in 1806. Benjamin was a follower of Bulfinch, and in 1803 listed himself in a Boston city directory as a "housewright." In the book, however, he termed himself an "Architect and Carpenter," and in every respect Benjamin was a professional. Through six editions, the last issued in 1826, he promulgated Adamesque principles of design. The book reflects a background in Georgian architecture and anticipates, particularly in the last edition, the coming of Greek Revival. But taken as a whole, it is about as coherent and as cogent a statement of a particular style as can be found in American architectural literature of the early nineteenth century. Benjamin was concerned with every aspect of the building, and includes in addition to basic information on the classical orders, designs for entrances, cornices, friezes, ornamental stucco ceilings, doors and sash, and windows. His advice on the use of mouldings is expressive of his aesthetic judgment and taste: "An assemblage of essential parts and mouldings is termed a profile; and on the choice, dispositions, and proportions of these depend the beauty or deformity of the composition. The most perfect profiles are such as consist of few mouldings, varied both in form and size, fitly applied with regard to their uses, and so distributed that the straight and curved ones succeed each other alternately."

Benjamin's principles of design and those of other Federal-style builders are outlined in a series of plans which are found in *The American Builder's Companion*. The plan and elevation for a small town house (Plate LI) is illustrated here. This is a four-story brick building of twelve rooms, excluding the kitchen and cellar floor. As noted, it is liberally supplied with fireplaces, central heating still being a dream of the future. The chimneys are positioned on the wall ends. The roof is low-pitched and is finished off by a simple entablature of brick with a projecting cornice. Windows are recessed on the main floor below semicircular arches and were probably intended to have double sash of six and six lights. The same arched treatment is given the front entrance, the space above undoubtedly intended to be fitted with a fanlight. Windows on the second floor are the same size as those of the first; on the third (or servants') floor, the windows are considerably smaller.

This was a modest city dwelling—not a tenement as the term is understood today, but certainly not a mansion. A family living in such a building might have had two servants, and their needs are provided for in the kitchen and cellar floor and in the upper chamber or third floor. Note, however, that there is only one stairwell in the interior, and the stairways themselves are not of the grand sort. The feeling throughout the dwelling, nevertheless, is of formal good taste. The graceful iron railings of the front stepped entryway express this grasp of the appropriate. The interior decoration of this dwelling was not described by Benjamin. Most certainly it was finished in a restrained manner with a minimum of decorative millwork, chimney pieces of a straightforward nature, and perhaps ornamental stucco ceilings in the principal rooms. Larger houses in the same style would be more elaborately appointed and would feature in mill- and plasterwork such classical forms as urns, pedestals, and rosettes, and motifs such as acanthus leaves, grapevines, and musical, patriotic, and agricultural trophies. As is evident from the design for a country house (Plate LV), provision was made for two formal rooms on the principal floor and for a grand staircase and a service backstairs.

Surviving examples of Federal architecture should be treated with the care given any national treasure. Perhaps not since the founding of the nation has such thoughtful attention been given to fashioning an architectural environment which is consistently well-designed and unified. That this was primarily the work of carpenter-builders with little formal architectural training merely increases the respect which is due these examples of their work.

Small town house, Asher Benjamin, Plate LI of
The American Builder's Companion

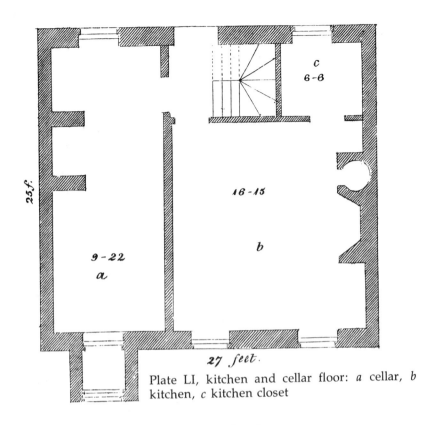

25 f.

9 - 22

a

16 - 15

b

c
6 - 6

27 feet.

Plate LI, kitchen and cellar floor: *a* cellar, *b* kitchen, *c* kitchen closet

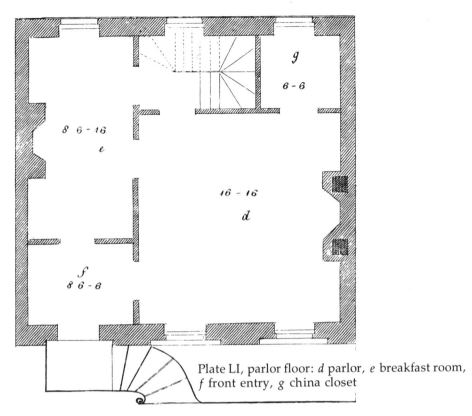

8 6 - 16

e

g
6 - 6

16 - 16

d

f
8 6 - 6

Plate LI, parlor floor: *d* parlor, *e* breakfast room, *f* front entry, *g* china closet

Plate LI, chamber floor

Plate LI, upper chamber floor

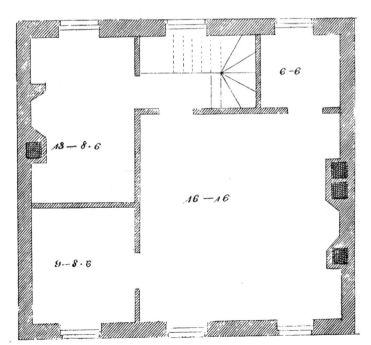

13 — 8 · 6

6 · 6

16 — 16

9 — 8 · 6

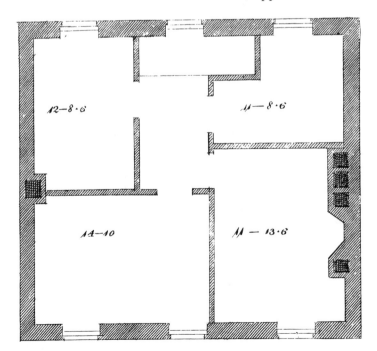

12 — 8 · 6

11 — 8 · 6

14 — 10

11 — 13 · 6

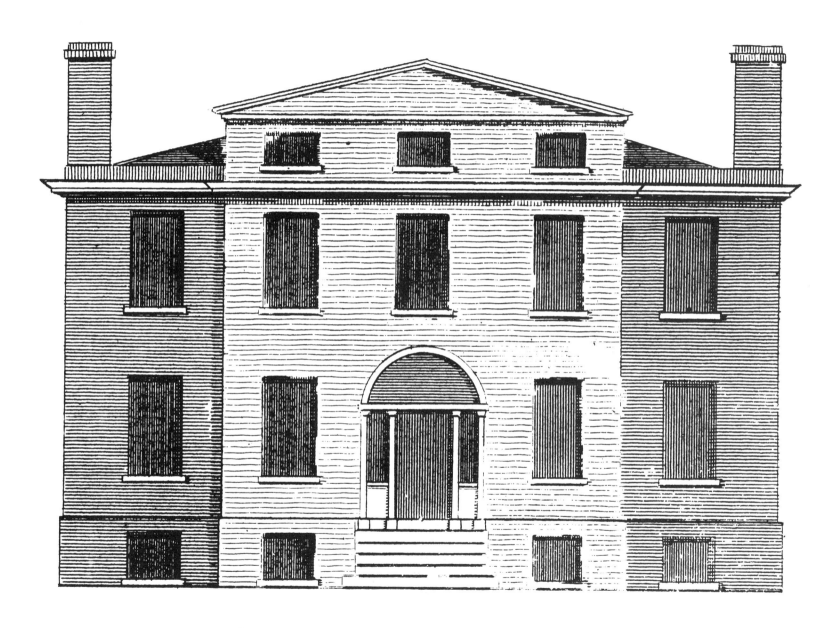

Country house, Asher Benjamin, Plate LV of *The American Builder's Companion*

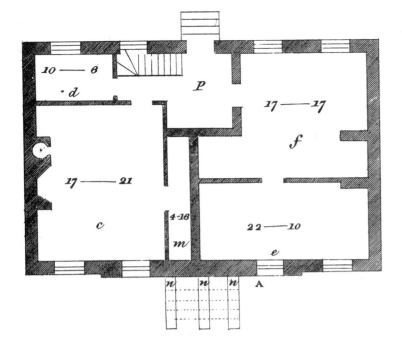

Plate LV, basement floor: *c* kitchen, *d* store-room, *e,f* cellar, *m* kitchen closet, *n,n,n* foundation of steps, *p* entry and back stairs

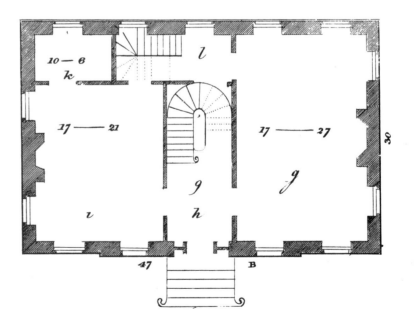

Plate LV, principal floor: *g* drawing room, *h* front entry and stairway, *i* parlor, *k* china closet, *l* back stairs and entry

The Greek Revival Style

No two homes in America have been as celebrated and slavishly imitated as Washington's Mount Vernon and Scarlett O'Hara's Tara. Both are Southern plantation mansions which impress the viewer with a feeling of classical grandeur. Washington's country house, however, was but a rural villa until the addition of a two-story colonnaded porch and of wings at each end in 1784-85. It is the columned, neoclassical image of Mount Vernon which has been treasured by generations. In the late eighteenth century the orders of Roman and Greek architecture were avidly studied by architects and builders. From this time until the mid-nineteenth century, the neoclassical spirit in architecture swept from East to Far West, from Maine to the Deep South. Mount Vernon's grand colonnade was to serve as a model for similar piazzas or porches which dignified and romanticized the façades of such Greek Revival plantation homes as Tara and its real-life counterparts from the 1820s until the 1860s.

The first stage of the classical revival in the last years of the eighteenth century and first decade of the nineteenth were devoted primarily to the use of Roman models of Greek orders, particularly the Corinthian. Much of the public architecture of the period reflects a fascination with Roman monumentality that was particularly appropriate for "governmental" purposes. The simpler style of pure Greek origin, however, soon replaced that of the Roman, particularly in home building. The Greek temple form, albeit very formal, could be interpreted in modest ways, and the Ionic and Doric orders were the preferred modes throughout America. "The boldness of the Grecian Doric," Asher Benjamin wrote in 1827, "attracts the attention of the spectator by the grandeur and fine proportion of its parts, the form of its mouldings, and the beautiful variety of light and shade on their surfaces, which greatly relieves them from each other, and renders their contour distinct to the eye."

Guides to building in the Greek style were widely circulated throughout the land. Benjamin's *The Practice of Architecture* (1833) and *The Practical House Carpenter* (1830) went through many editions. The handbooks of Minard Lafever, *The Beauties of Modern Architecture* (1835) and *The Modern Builder's Guide* (1833), were also persuasive and useful compilations of designs. With such directions in hand, the reasonably skilled carpenter-builder in the Western Reserve of Ohio, the plains of Georgia, or other far-distant territories could fashion rather handsome one- or two-story homes.

The most typical of such structures are those which faithfully reproduce the temple façade, the round or square columns being constructed of wood, brick or stone. Those of the Doric order are simple fluted forms which are topped with a plain cushion capital, architrave, frieze panel, and cornice. The Ionic column is fitted in a capital with large volutes or spiral scrolls and ends in architrave, frieze, and cornice. The Corinthian column is the most elaborate and least encountered in American domestic building. The capital is shaped in the form of an inverted bell and contains volutes and two or three rows of acanthus leaves. The cornice and the rest of the entablature is richly ornamented.

Despite the availability of uniform specifications for such buildings, no two are exactly alike. Over time distinct variant forms developed regionally. In the North the columns were often tucked into the façade as pilasters. In the South the portico was deepened and sometimes even wrapped around three sides of the structure. A second-floor balcony with ornamental ironwork railings was often added across the front. Northern houses tended to be rather prim and proper; those of the South, more open and inviting.

Almost all Greek Revival residences do share some characteristic features. These include a low-pitched roof, frieze or pierced grille windows at what would be the attic level below the architrave band, cornices with dentils, Greek key fret ornamentation, broad architrave trim around doors and windows, and columned entryways with a rectangular transom and sidelights.

The basic temple profile of Greek Revival in the North is illustrated in the Judge Wilson house, Ann Arbor, Michigan, built in the 1830s. The columns are Ionic and are surmounted by a very simple entablature. The pediment is composed of what is termed a raking cornice which also includes dentils. The front windows are quite narrow and elongated. The three bays they form perfectly complement the four-columned portico.

The interior of this rectangular structure is divided into four principal rooms on the first floor and a similar number on the second. As the floor plan indicates, the entryway and hall are positioned at one side, and rooms are lined up in a rather static fashion one after the other. Form has dictated function to perhaps a monotonous degree. The decorative mouldings of windows, fireplaces, and door surrounds, however, soften the formal air. This woodwork matches that of the exterior in its simplicity. Working fireplaces are provided in nearly all rooms.

Whereas many Greek Revival homes in the Midwest and East are asymmetrical in arrangement of doors and windows and interior divisions of space, some do provide a center entry and seek to break up the box-like perspective by use of an L- or T-shaped floor plan. Southern Greek Revival residences are more likely to present a variety of forms and elements which enliven the basic neoclassical formula. These homes resemble in some respects a Georgian Colonial mansion with dormer windows and a balustrade breaking the roof line of a temple house aligned in the Mount Vernon manner. As noted earlier, ornamental balconies are frequently introduced at the second-floor level. The interior of such dwellings is similar to that found in the late Colonial with a wide center hall providing access to two formal front rooms—parlor and living room—and two rear rooms. In many Southern homes, cooking and other work performed by servants was centered on a basement level that was at least partially above ground.

Greek Revival homes of all sorts reflect intelligent planning and sound aesthetic judgment often missing in domestic American architecture. If there is a fault to be found in the style, it is the lack of spontaneity which led to the encasing of home life in a strict structural framework. Such early critics of Greek Revival as Andrew Jackson Downing found the formality stultifying and depressing and embraced instead a freer Gothic style which, in time, was to prevail throughout the century in one form or another. In their pursuit of the "picturesque," however, these champions of a new aesthetic failed to recognize the same qualities in many Greek Revival homes. Southerners were the last to give up their antebellum manners and modes. And "the more in ruin," Vincent Scully has commented, "the more Greek" their mansions seemed to be. If tragedy had been played out against a Northern backdrop, perhaps the neoclassical temples of good taste and propriety would have acquired a more tragic and therefore romantic image.

Judge Wilson House, Ann Arbor, Michigan, c. 1836

Parlor, Wilson House

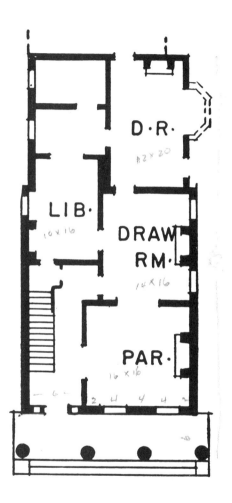

First floor, Wilson House

21

RICHARDSON. SC.

"Grecian Cottage," New Jersey, from William H. Ranlett, *The Architect* (1851)

René Beauregard House, Chalmette, Louisiana, mid-nine-teenth century

The Gothic Style

The cottage enjoyed a popularity in the New World far beyond that achieved in rural England. Often defined as a "small rustic" structure, this kind of building served the needs of many social classes, including workmen and country gentlemen. Despite popular misconception, a cottage can be a quite large, imposing structure, as were many built in North America and Great Britain during the first half of the nineteenth century. In general, however, this type of house was built on a small scale. As conceived by Andrew Jackson Downing, Andrew Jackson Davis, and Richard Upjohn, it was designed in the Gothic style, and expressed much in the way of romantic "feeling," to use one of Downing's favorite terms. "Now, every cottage may not display *science* or knowledge," he wrote in *The Architecture of Country Houses* (1850), "because science demands architectural education in its builder or designer, as well as, in many cases, some additional expense. But *feeling* may be evinced by every one possessing it. . . ." The Gothic style cottage in America was a simple, democratic, and pleasantly liveable building form that suited the needs of a people seeking a change from the formal and aristocratic Federal and Greek Revival styles.

Simple domestic dwellings such as the Downing cottage illustrated here are often termed "Carpenter Gothic." Most are the work of carpenter/builders and not architects. Almost all display the kind of fancy woodwork which we automatically call "gingerbread"—finials, verge or bargeboards, brackets, canopies. For Downing, however, the terms "Carpenter Gothic" and "gingerbread" were anathematic. The architectural elements which he suggested provided "feeling," a "softening and humanizing expression," and were of the hand and not the machine-made sort. "All ornaments which are not simple," Downing wrote, "and cannot be executed in a substantial and appropriate manner, should at once be rejected; all flimsy and meager decorations which have a pasteboard effect, are as unworthy of, and unbecoming for the house of him who understands the true beauty of a cottage life, as glass breastpins or gilt-pewter spoons would be for his personal ornaments or family service of plate." Unfortunately, not all followers of Downing (or the many other exponents of the cottage style) shared his love of quality and appropriateness. They were, however, unanimous in their appreciation of the outlines of the new style.

Cottages in the Downing style, many copied directly from his pattern books, first appeared in the Hudson Valley and Northeast and gradually emerged as far west as California in prefabricated form. Design II, a "small bracketed cottage," is one of the simplest of the Downing forms to be presented in *The Architecture of Country Houses*. It displays many of the very basic elements of country Gothic design—the use of vertical board walls, a steep gable roof, diamond-paned sashes, a bay window, handsomely finished chimney tops, and brackets over windows and doors. Downing felt that vergeboards were appropriate only for a villa, but he did use them in fancier cottage designs. "A bay window," he wrote, "does not of necessity belong to a small cottage [but it] raises the character of such a cottage wherever it is simple and tastefully introduced."

Downing, not trained as an architect, was led to take up the design of houses by an interest in the art of landscaping. As one of the accompanying illustrations shows, the lack of any kind of greenery renders the structure characterless. Downing has exaggerated the difference by eliminating certain touches around the windows, the bracketed vine-canopy over the front window to the left, and by showing the house without a view of the side bay window. Also gone are the "little rustic arbors or covered seats" on each side of the bay window which, in his words, "convey . . . an impression of refinement and taste attained in that simple manner so appropriate to a small cottage."

The inner spaces are arranged in as workable and attractive a manner as is possible in a modest home. The living room is clearly separated from the other ground-floor rooms and is provided with a pleasant bay-window nook, a fireplace, and two ample closets on each side of the fireplace. This room is designed as a proper parlor. "The real living room of the family," Downing explained, "will, in great measure, be also the kitchen . . .; [it] will be used as a back-kitchen for the rough-work, washing, etc., so that in summer, and indeed at any time, the living room can be made to have the comfortable aspect of a cottage parlor, by confining the rough-work to the kitchen proper." A lean-to addition on the back provides for storage of coal on one side and a pantry on the other with a separate outside kitchen entrance inbetween. The second or chamber floor is neatly divided into three sleeping areas, two of which are supplied with flues for stove pipes. These rooms,

"Small Bracketed Cottage," Andrew Jackson Downing, Design II, Figs. 9 and 11 of *The Architecture of Country Houses* (1850).

Brackets are the projections above the doors. There seem to be more above the windows

The bay window is "square"

vergeboards or bargeboards - almost used to cover rafters

Both used to cover rafters extending beyond gable

because of the steep roof lines, are considerably less spacious than those below.

Architectural critics today loudly lament the lack of well-designed plans for modest homes, and they are right. The characterless boxes which pass for places of repose are a far cry from those picturesque cottages with "feeling" popularized by Downing and his contemporaries. The small, romantic Gothic touches added to these buildings immeasurably increased their personal and real value.

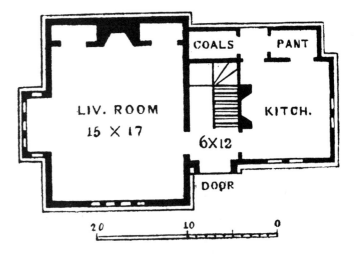

Principal floor, Design II, Fig. 10

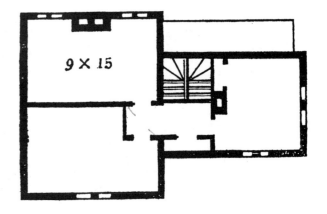

Chamber floor, Design II, Fig. 12

Cottage, Design XI, Henry W. Cleaveland, William Backus, and Samuel D. Backus, *Village and Farm Cottages* (1856). This mid-century design, termed by the authors "compact and economical" anticipates the one-and-a-half story bungalow of the late 1800s.

Gothic Revival parlor, from Henry W. Cleaveland, William
Backus, and Samuel D. Backus, *Village and Farm Cottages* (1856)

"English Cottage," William H. Ranlett, Design XLIV of *The Architect* (1851)

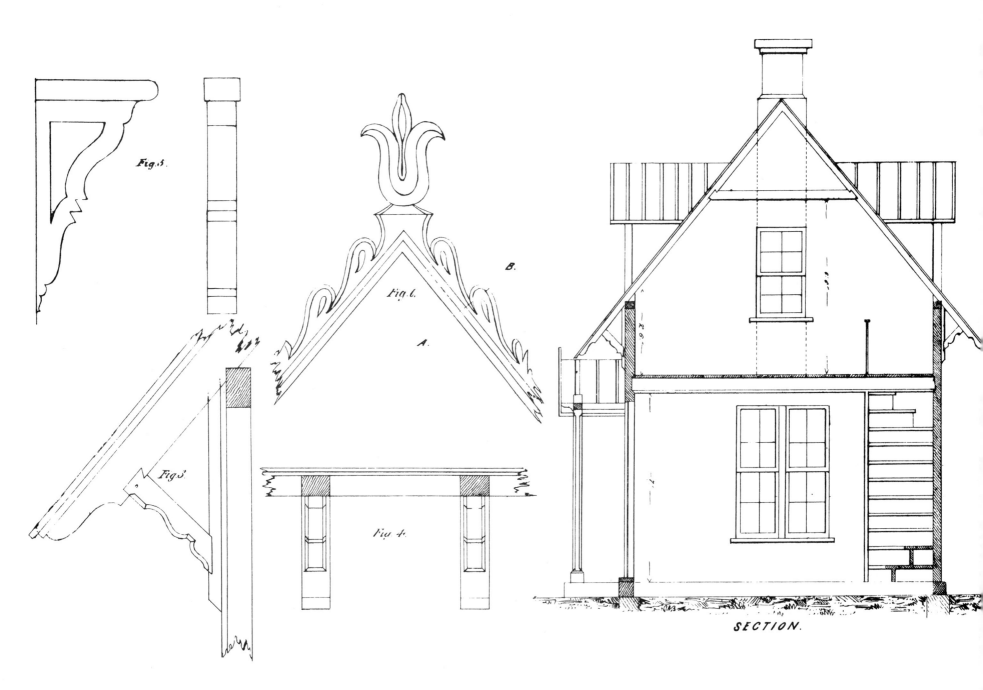

Fig. 5.

Fig. 6.

B.

A.

Fig. 3.

Fig. 4.

SECTION.

Details and section, "English Cottage"

"Rural Gothic Villa," Andrew Jackson Downing, Design XXIX,
Figure 148 of *The Architecture of Country Houses* (1850).

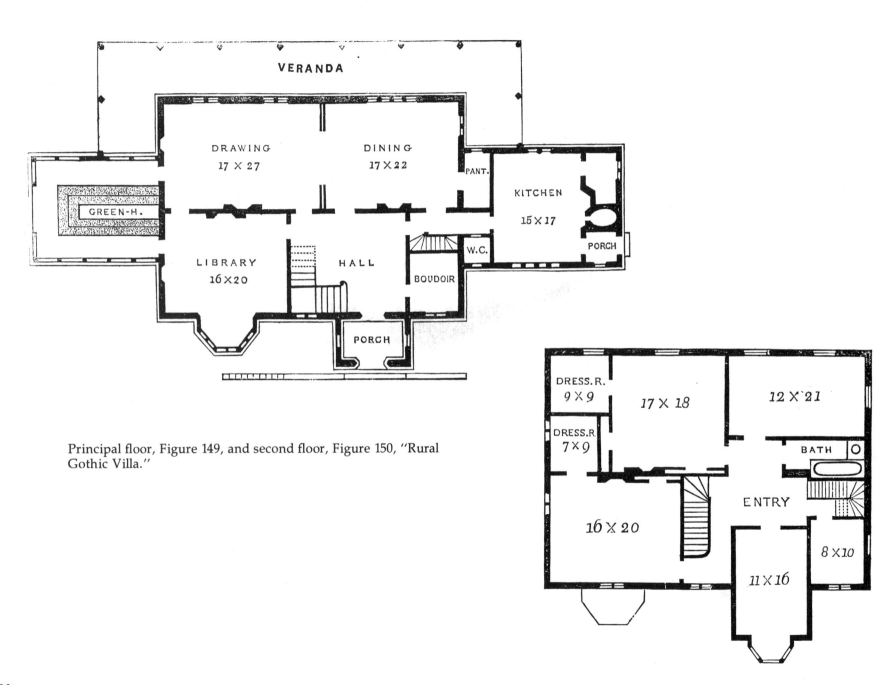

VERANDA

DRAWING
17 × 27

DINING
17 × 22

PANT.

KITCHEN
15 × 17

GREEN-H.

W.C.

PORCH

LIBRARY
16 × 20

HALL

BOUDOIR

PORCH

DRESS. R.
9 × 9

17 × 18

12 × 21

DRESS. R.
7 × 9

BATH

16 × 20

ENTRY

8 × 10

11 × 16

Principal floor, Figure 149, and second floor, Figure 150, "Rural Gothic Villa."

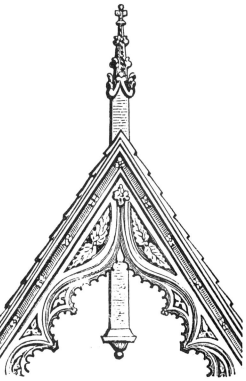

Elevation and plan of window, Figure 152, bay window, Figure 153, and vergeboard, Figure 154, "Rural Gothic Villa."

The Italianate Style

No term can adequately describe the American fashion for the classical and picturesque in architecture and landscaping during the mid-nineteenth century. "The Italianate" is as broad a term as can be applied to the romantic style of a non-Gothic sort which appeared first in the Northeast. Some have called it Tuscan; others, Anglo-Italian. Architect John Notman's 1837 house for Bishop Doane at Burlington, New Jersey, was, to all intents, an Italian villa not unlike those found in the Tuscan countryside. Andrew Jackson Downing popularized Notman's design and those of Andrew Jackson Davis in two popular books of the period, *Cottage Residences* (1842) and *The Architecture of Country Houses* (1850). Other architects such as William H. Ranlett also sought to spread the word of the new style which had first gained popularity in England. In volume II of his series of designs (1851), Ranlett argues that the Anglo-Italian "might with greater propriety be called the American-Italian, for it is more purely American than Italian in character, and hardly at all resembles the English style of villas." Although relatively faithful to European models, even the first Italianate houses built for innovative and wealthy clients lacked the elaborate decoration and appointments of the Old World. Such "richness," according to Ranlett, "would ill accord with the severity of our republican habits, and that predominance of economy and comfort which so distinctly mark all the efforts of American art."

The American structure was distinguished primarily by the use of projecting eaves and heavy supporting brackets. By no means was campanile or tower a basic ingredient in the design. Again, Ranlett explained and rationalized away the differences between the new and old: "The pure Italian villas and palatial residences have a monumental character, imparted by their regular proportioned tablature, which our so-called Anglo-Italian villas with their bracketed eaves must lack. These projecting eaves, so becoming in our sunny climate, and their supporting brackets impart to a country house an aspect of cheerfulness and comfort which more than compensates for the lack of classic beauty occasioned by the absence of the regularly proportioned cornice of the Italian villa." Such eaves, one would think today, would serve just as admirably in sunny Tuscany. But Ranlett had a point: the American Italianate style was as valid and becoming as any derivative fashion could be. By the late 1850s such discussions of stylistic purity were largely academic; the general public knew only of houses in the "Italian order" or "manner."

The basic rectangular profile of the American home was not appreciably changed by the advent of the Italianate. Some of the early designs, as Ranlett's plate 33 illustrates, make use of an "L"-shaped floor plan; others employ the "T." Later homes were more likely to assume a standard box-like shape. All, however, make use of broad eaves and brackets, the latter often found in pairs. The roofs are generally of the low hip variety and slope very gently. Windows are much narrower than those found in houses of an earlier style and are often paired or even grouped in threes. Some windows are circular-headed. A three-story tower or campanile might be found angled at a corner of the structure or set to one side of the main part of the façade. The use of the balcony, veranda loggia, cupola, and belvidere and bay windows further accentuate the picturesque qualities of an Italianate house.

A study of elevations and floor plans will suggest something of an architect's intention to introduce interest in a house by incorporating balconies and a veranda. This was also accomplished by placing such major structural forms as a tower at an arresting angle to the main house. As historian Vincent Scully has noted, "Picturesque buildings were meant to unfold to the viewer over time, as he approached them along the contrived curves of their site plans or, inside, wandered from room to room according to an asymmetrical pattern which created the affect of freedom and discovery." This sense of the unusual and expansive would have been experienced by a visitor to the Ranlett house which, in terms of its dimensions, was truly a modest structure. He would first ascend the steps to the veranda and then turn to the left to the main entryway in the angled tower. Upon entering the tower, he would be led to the parlor which is set at an acute angle from the reception area.

The imaginative Ranlett design was to be executed in brick and then stuccoed. Cut brownstone was specified for sills, lintels, and the chimney top. The very low roof was to be of tin plates. The floor plan provides for four wood-burning fireplaces—one in the cellar, not shown; one in the parlor; a cooking fireplace in the kitchen; and a fourth in the upper "chamber." The mantels for these were to be wood except for that of the parlor which called for marble. This room was further ornamented with a moulded plaster cor-

Broad eaves heavy supporting brackets

"Italian Villa," William H. Ranlett, Design XXXIII of *The Architect* (1851).

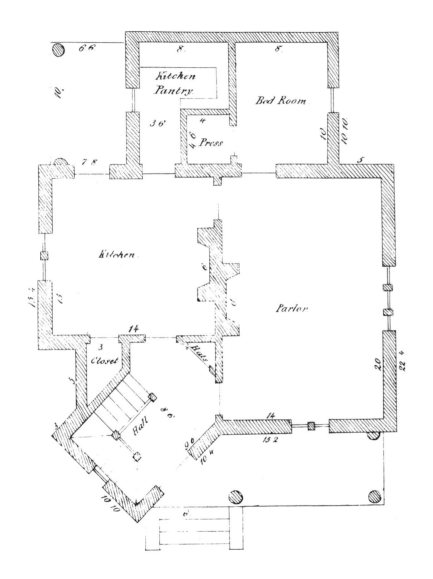

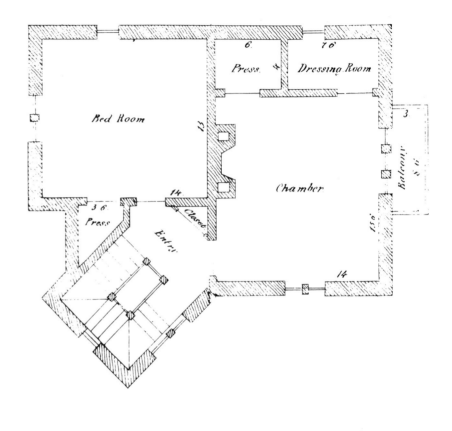

First and second stories, "Italian Villa."

nice. Sketches of the millwork needed for the cornices and the exterior balconies are shown in plate XXIV, figures 4 and 5.

Not all builders or architects working in the Italianate Style were as skilled as Ranlett in introducing romantic qualities. In this respect, the second house plan of 1858 is probably more representative of American building design of the time. Although it is not as interesting a structure as those of Ranlett, it has a charm and substance which recommended it then and heighten its interest now. A description of the house appeared in the *American Agriculturist* in 1859 and supplies us with some information on the colors, building materials, and those special details which make a house a home.

The average Italianate structure was box-like, and its front entrance was set off by a columned portico or veranda. A majority were of wood and not of brick. Some featured a rectangular window or two on the first floor. In these respects, this second house is a model home. The interior features of the house are also typical. The most imposing structural element is the spiral staircase reached from a generously-spaced front hall. Folding doors open the parlor and library to the hall and, according to the writer, allow one to enjoy a "view across the suite of rooms, from one bay window to the other [which] is quite agreeable and striking." Decorative details include elaborate mouldings in the principal first-floor rooms, moulded panel doors (also seen in the entryway), the use of imitation wood graining in the hall, butternut or similar wood paneling (in the library), and light-colored wallpapers in the parlor and dining room.

The last word in the description is devoted to the nine-foot veranda, which "being furnished with settees, and shaded by honeysuckles and the American ivy, furnishes pleasant resort throughout almost every day in Summer." The mid-Victorian, seeking respite from the energetic pace of commercial American society, could hardly envision anything more satisfying.

Balcony details, "Italian Villa."

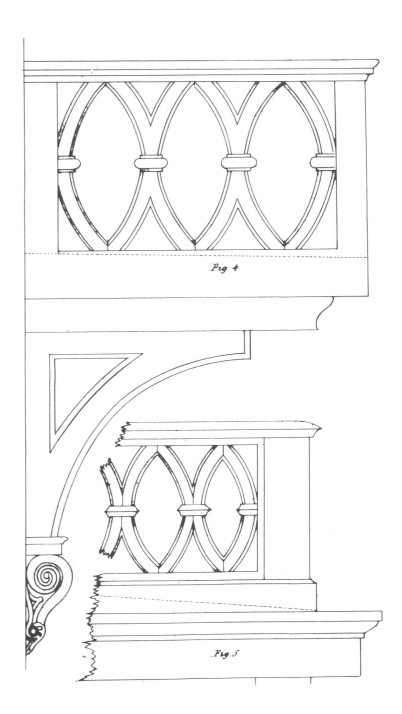

Fig. 4

Fig. 5

"Dwelling house in the Italian Order," *American Agriculturist*
(1859).

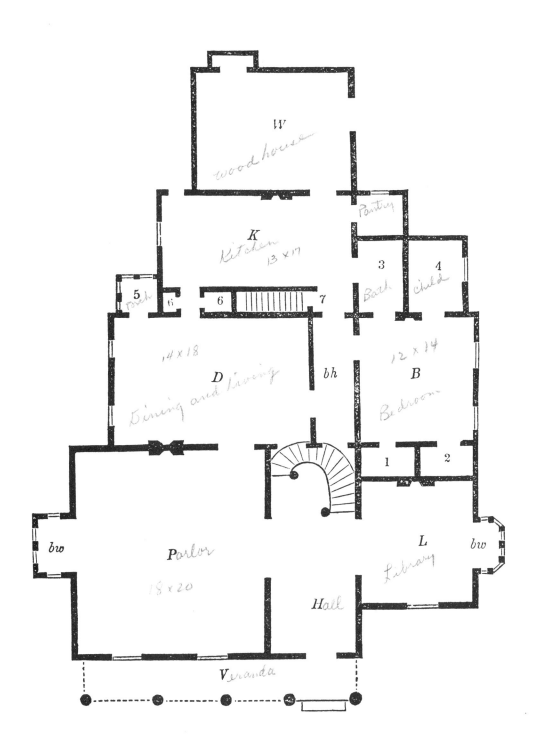

Principal floor, "Dwelling House in the Italian Order": *B* bedroom, 12 × 14; *bh* back hall; *bw* bay window; *D* dining and living room, 14 × 18; *H* front hall; *K* kitchen, 13 × 17; *L* library, 12 × 13; *P* parlor, 18 × 20; *V* veranda; *W* wood house; *1,2* closet; *3* bathroom, *4* child's room; *5* covered porch to living room; *6,6* china closets; *7* back stairs; *8* pantry and storeroom.

Above, "Plain Interior, Grecian Style," Figure 175; *below*, "Dining Room, Italian Style," Figure 176, Andrew Jackson Downing, *The Architecture of Country Houses* (1850). In Downing's mind there was no doubt about the aesthetic improvement apparent in the more picturesque Italian mode.

"Villa in the Italian Style," Andrew Jackson Downing, Design XXVIII of *The Architecture of Country Houses* (1850).

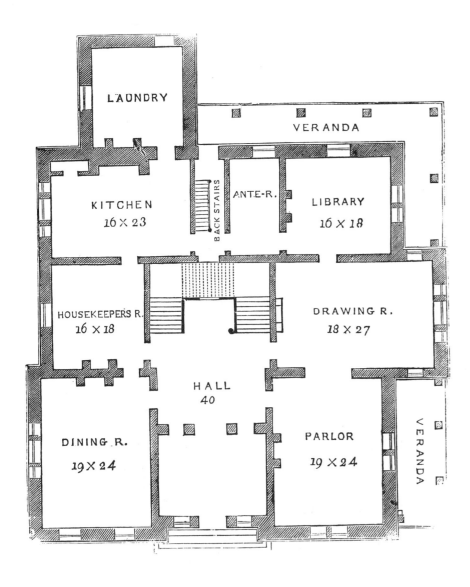

Principal floor, Figure 144, "Villa in the Italian
Style."

Balcony window, Figure 145, "Villa in the Italian Style."

"Double House in the Italian Style," front elevation, William H. Ranlett, Design XLIII of *The Architect* (1851).

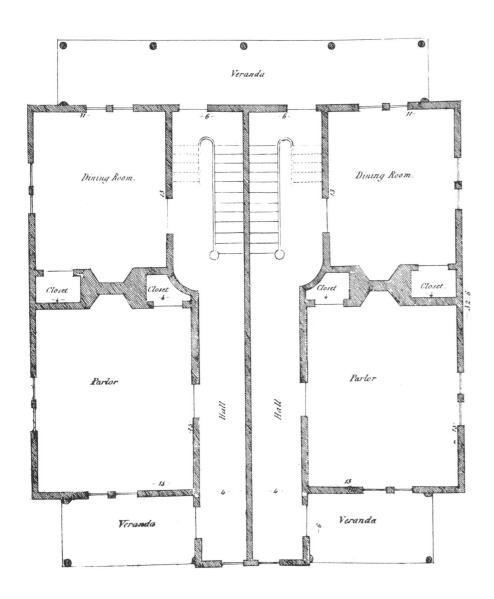

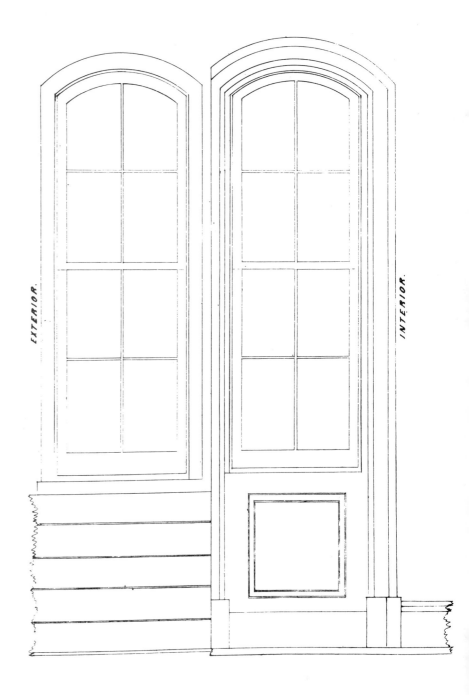

Principal story and exterior and interior window details, "Double House in the Italian Style."

The Second Empire or Mansard Style

1860-1880

Homes in this style, popular during the years from 1860 to 1880, have won renewed appreciation only recently. Indubitably Victorian, such structures suggest much that was overstuffed and mannered in the mid- to late-nineteenth century. The Mansard style has also been called the General Grant style, a not unfitting designation for an architectural form which suited the needs of the bourgeoisie of the Gilded Age. The felicities of the Mansard style are not to be found in scale or ornament. These were somewhat top-heavy, lumbering structures. What then is there to celebrate? A great number of such buildings—public and domestic—exhibit a refreshing degree of imaginative eclecticism. The juxtaposition of a towering center pavilion against the mass of the mansarded structure, the use of sweeping porches or piazzas, the generous display of various building materials such as slate, tin, and wood—these elements are worthy of study and preservation. Such features are exhibited in the Flushing, New York, home illustrated here, and in such nationally-acclaimed civic structures as the Boston City Hall, Philadelphia's City Hall, and the Executive Office Building in Washington, D.C.

Directly or indirectly, American architects were influenced by the design of the extension to the Louvre in Paris (1852-57). The central architectural landmark of the Second Empire of Napoleon III, it was first copied in England as a fitting model for monumental public buildings. The first Grand Central Depot in New York (1869-71), designed by Isaac C. Buckhout and J. B. Snook, was a splendid palace in the Mansard mode with three square-domed pavilions, and the New Louvre was its inspiration.

It was long thought that the term "Mansard" owes its origin to the French architect François Mansart (1598-1666), the original designer of the Louvre, but this attribution is questioned today. The word "mansarde" in French, however, does mean a garret or attic and there can be no mistaking the style of a house with a top floor which is described in French as *mansardé*. Adoption of the mansard was not merely a stylistic gesture but was, as well, a utilitarian improvement: the pitch of the average mansard roof allows for greater use of attic space for living purposes. The slope of nearly every mansard roof, of course, is broken by dormer windows. The slope of the roof varies greatly from building to building. The majority form straight angles, but others curve convexly or concavely. In almost every case, the roof is clearly delineated from the mass of the building by a bracketed cornice. Chimneys are given considerable prominence and are often capped in a highly ornamental fashion. Windows, too, are frequently given decorative relief in the form of curved heads described as "eye-brow." The windows may be curved or rectilinear, and are often paired.

Details such as these are reflected in the country house built in the mid-1860s in Flushing, then an area of rural residences. The home was built for speculation by Orange Judd, one of the publishers of the popular monthly *American Agriculturist*, and extensively described in the magazine. The dominant architectural features of the house are a central pavilion of Italianate inspiration and a slightly concave mansard slope of blue slate; the flat top is covered with tin. One enters the house from a wide piazza extending the width of the structure. The rooms on the first floor are 11½ feet high and are reached through a center hall 8½ feet wide and three times as long. According to the description, "A wide spacious hall is desirable. The appearance of this to one first entering a house gives an impression of the whole building that is not overcome. If wide, there is a feeling of size and substantial comfort, no matter how small the individual rooms may be. One does not get over the idea that there is plenty of room somewhere in the house."

Indeed there is. This is a three-story home with basement. The basement contains the coal-burning furnace, storage areas, and kitchen. The first floor provides for a main parlor, library, sitting room or family parlor (today's "family room"), dining room, and butler's pantry. On the second story are found a minimum of five bedrooms, one of which could be used, the builder suggests, as a sewing or nurse's room, and a family-sized bathroom. The attic or third story includes three bedrooms which are fitted with dormer windows. A tower room or observatory is reached by a staircase from a small room which can be used as a bedroom or storeroom. As noted on the floor plan, the third story also houses the water tank. This feature is simply explained: "A house anywhere in the country can have an abundant supply of the best 'distilled' water—the purest possible. Nature carries it up; we have only to provide for interrupting it as it comes down. Forty to fifty barrels will furnish ample supply from one rain storm to another. In case of a long drought, the force-pump will readily fill the tank."

As in so many period houses of the eighteenth and nineteenth centuries, this dwelling made provision for the work

Orange Judd House, Flushing, New York, *American Agriculturist* (1866).

and housing of servants. A mid-nineteenth century dwelling of this standing was likely to be equipped with certain conveniences such as bell pulls and speaking tubes for the summoning of those in service. "Houses thus fitted up command good 'help,' and less of it, and save the housewife immense labor and worry." The duties undoubtedly included shoveling coal for the furnace, and the cleaning of gas fixtures which were found in every room. Each room was also supplied with two ventilators, one near the baseboard and the second close to the ceiling, for the reception and expelling of forced hot air. The main parlor, the family parlor, and three second-story bedrooms were supplied with fireplaces. These were fitted with Italian marble mantels, summer pieces, and German-silver guards.

The interior decoration of the dwelling is not extensively discussed, but some mention of colors is made. The exterior, in keeping with many mid-Victorian dwellings, was painted a light gray with darker shadings of this color for details. As many researchers have learned from paint analysis in recent years, the Victorians did not, for the most part, use a strongly contrasting color for details. Most of the bedrooms were painted a dead white. Two of the principal first floor rooms are stipple grained in imitation of walnut; the main parlor is painted in "shaded" white with a bluish-gray tint used on portions of the mouldings. The profile of the cornice mouldings used on the various stories is illustrated here.

Various details of this house, excepting the Italianate-style tower, are commonly found in Second Empire or Mansard dwellings of stone, brick, and wood. These were built in all areas of the United States with varying degrees of success. The center pavilion was most often capped with a steeply-sloped mansard roof, the top of which was decorated with iron cresting. Other ironwork may have been used in balustraded fashion to crown the lower roof. The sides of the mansard roofs themselves may have been laid with slates of various colors in an interesting design, or with tin plates. The Judd house cost $12,000 to build, an expensive project at the time, and it is evident that only fine materials were used. It provided for twenty-one closets and pantries. This attention to comfort and convenience cannot be indulged in the same way today, but then the mid-Victorians could not partake of the many "necessities" of the electric and electronic age. Today, when second thought is being given to the true utility of our fossil-fueled conveniences of kitchen and utility room, the extravagances indulged in the 1860s—commodious porches, handsomely-finished fireplaces, deep closets, and such an imaginative nook as the observatory—assume a much less eccentric profile.

First Story.

Second Story.

Third Story.

Interior casings or trimmings, Judd House.

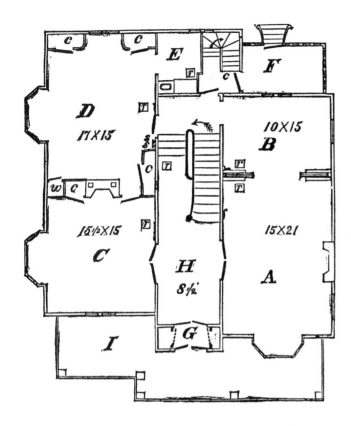

First story, Judd House: *A* main parlor, *B* library, *C* family parlor, *D* dining room, *E* butler's pantry, *F* rear piazza, *g* vestibule, *H* main hall, *I* front piazza, *c* closets, *r* warm air registers.

Second story, Judd House: *K,L,M,N* bedrooms, *O* bathroom, *P* main hall, *Q* dressing or sewing room, *R* rear stairs hall, *b* washbasins, *c* closets.

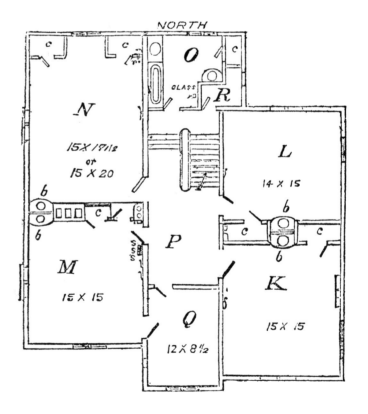

French roof villa, E. C. Hussey, Plate No. 28 of *Home Building* (1875). The cost of the home, if built in New York, was estimated at $7,500.

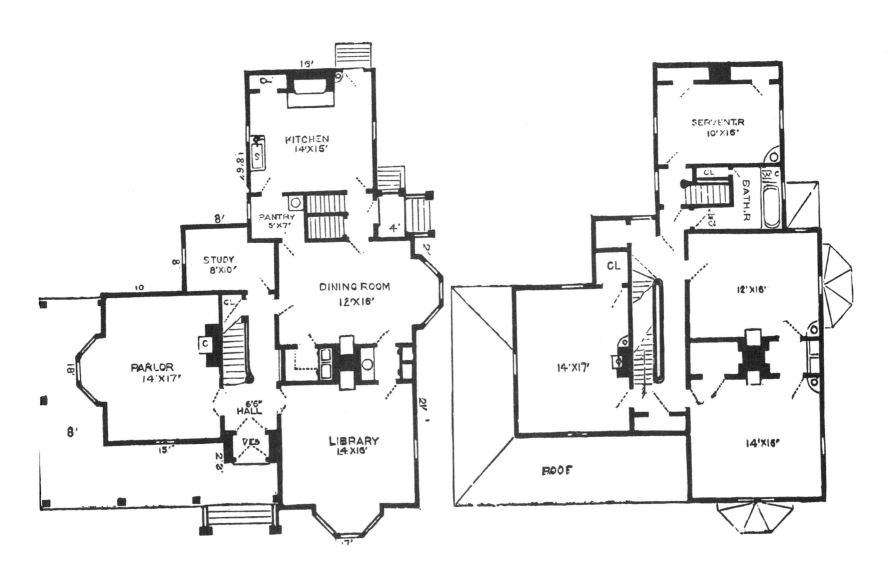

Ground and chamber plans, French roof villa.

"A Convenient Country or Village House," *left*, front or southeast elevation; *right*, rear or northwest elevation; *American Agriculturist* (1870). The residence was described as having "modern improvements"—gas lighting, hot and cold running water, bathroom, water closet, warm air furnace, speaking tubes, and dumbwaiters. The cost was estimated at $7,000 to $8,000.

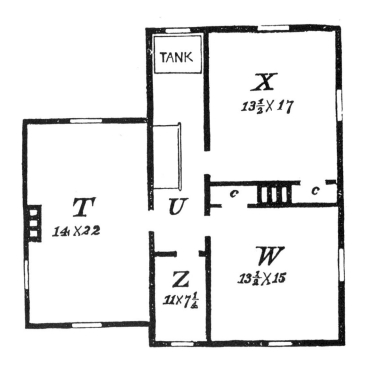

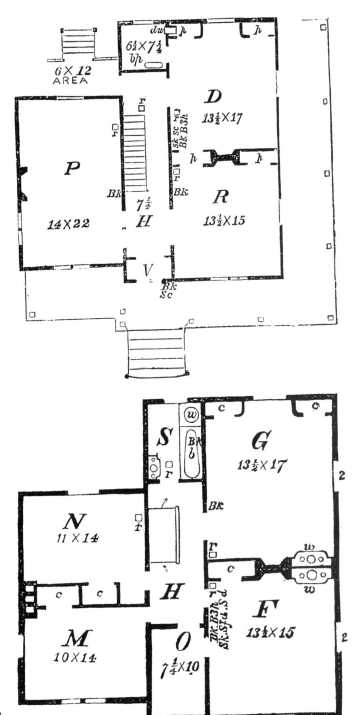

Upper left, first story, "A Convenient Country or Village House": *B3h,Bk* bell pull, *Bp* butler's pantry, *D* dining room, *dw* dumbwaiter, *H* main hall, *p* closet, *P* parlor, *r* warm air register, *R* reception or living room, *sc,sk* speaking tube, *V* vestibule; *lower left,* second story: *b* bathtub, *bk* bell pull, *c* closet, *F,G,M,N* bedroom, *H* hall, *O* dressing or sewing room, *r* warm air register, *S* bathroom, *Sk,Sf,Sfd* speaking tube, *w* washstand; *above,* third story: *T* exercise room, *U* hall, *W,X* bedroom, *Z* servant's room.

"Cheap Residence with French Roof," G. B. Croff, architect,
Fort Edward, New York, Plate 13 of *Bicknell's Village Builder*
(1872). The estimated building cost was $4,000.

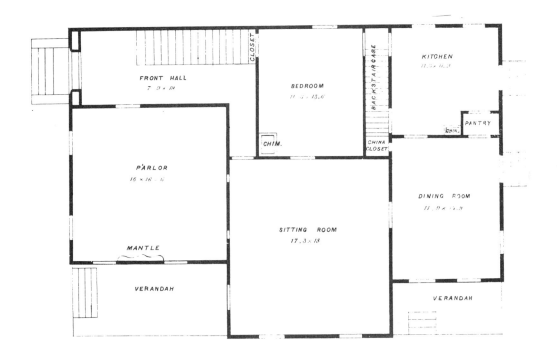

First and second floors, "Cheap Residence with
French Roof."

The Stick Style

1850 +

Like F. L. Wright

Cottages in the country were often built during the mid-nineteenth century in what critic Vincent Scully has termed "Stick Style." This was an early form of structuralism, and a particularly American phenomenon. The exterior clapboard walls of such wood frame buildings featured an overlay of vertical, horizontal, and diagonal boards which, however decorative in themselves, also served to emphasize the basic outline of gables, porches, and window openings. These were "picturesque" homes in the sense that Andrew Jackson Downing used the term, and he was largely responsible for the emergence of a "stick work" aesthetic in the 1850s and '60s. This was a truthful, honest style. "For Downing and his followers," Scully has explained, "it was the skeleton of the wooden frame whose expression 'reality' demanded. Hence, the American home visually shed its sheathing skin and clad itself in vertical boards and battens to express its vertical studs, and pushed out the light frames of porches as picturesque viewing platforms and as pretext for the visual exploitation of all the members of the frame."

Stick Style homes were often built at the seashore and were constructed by use of the balloon frame method at relatively low cost. By the 1850s it was possible for light-weight framing to be manufactured in almost mass-produced fashion, and, with the spread of an efficient transportation network, the various elements could be shipped far and wide. In *Palliser's New Cottage Homes* (1887) balloon framing is said to have "had its origin in the early settlement of our prairies where it was impossible to obtain heavy timbers and skillful mechanics, and its simple, effective and economical manner of construction has been of great benefit in building up new territory and sections of this country, and being stronger than any other method of framing has led to its universal adoption for buildings of every class throughout the United States."

Despite the fact that stick work emphasized the frame or structure and its varied elements, it often had an airy if not delicate feeling to it. This is a far cry from the half-timbering effects produced on later Queen Anne and English Tudor buildings. Such a structurally "honest" and decorative form is found in design 149 of *Palliser's New Cottage Homes*. It was intended for construction in Florida or anywhere along the sea coast as a summer vacation home. Note that the house is built on posts so as to admit, according to the architects, "free circulation of air." The overall design of the house is such as to allow "every opportunity of getting through the house all the breeze there may be about. . . ." This form of construction, naturally, also cut down greatly on cost. The wide front piazza and second-floor "porch room" provide not only welcome shaded areas but pleasant viewpoints from which to observe the pleasures of nature.

Yet another seashore design is that by William G. Preston of Boston reproduced in *Modern Architectural Designs and Details* (1881) by William T. Comstock. This much more substantial building reflects a greater dependence on then current Queen Anne decoration, especially in the use of fish-scale shingles. The overall composition, however, belongs to the Stick Style. This is reflected in the expansive veranda supported by diagonal braces and the gentle arches of the corner pavilion section. This latter element suggests an Oriental inspiration. Boards are also used diagonally against horizontal boards in the two-story gable at the front. Diagonal brackets appear to support this front gable and the dormer windows at the side. Framing plans are shown here in addition to the usual floor plans to give the reader some feeling for how the external finishing is reflective of the structural elements.

In keeping with the needs of a vacationing family, the exterior areas—veranda, terrace, and balcony—are nearly as large as the interior. Nearly every room on the first floor level opens up to the outside. On the second floor the balcony provides covered porch; dormers in two of the bedrooms project outward toward the sea. The layout of the rooms is a functional one, not without interest in its angular form, but, still, basically utilitarian.

The Stick Style has been termed by historian Marcus Whiffen "one of the two most purely American styles of the nineteenth century." Downing's vision of the realistic *and* the picturesque was most perfectly realized in the combining of board and batten with slender horizontal, vertical, and/or diagonal appliqués which followed the lines of framing. Wood—the most abundant building material in North America—could be shaped and used in ways not possible with less malleable mediums such as brick and stone, at least by the average home builder. The tortured fretwork which came from the jig saw is another matter. Such gingerbread has been considered the most distinctive expression of the Victorian in the building arts. This is not to deny its existence; more than sufficient examples exist of such amusing, but often poorly executed, ornamental work in every area of North America. Gingerbread, decried by Downing in

Left, side, and, *right*, front elevations, Design 149, Plate 51 of *Palliser's New Cottage Homes* (1887). The cost was estimated to be $1,000.

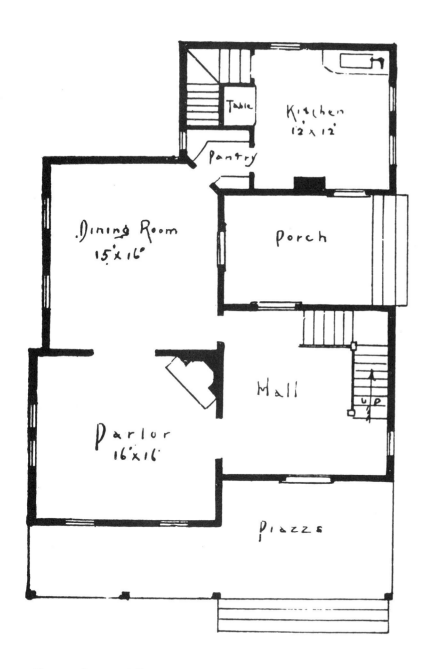

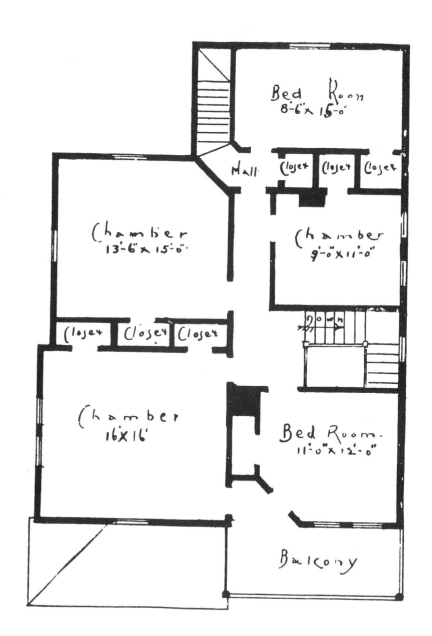

First and second floors, Design 149.

the 1840s and in its Queen Anne manifestations by its supposed progenitor, English designer Charles Eastlake, could be, in the words of Lewis Mumford, "a disguise for mean or thoughtless workmanship. . . ." As we have seen, decorative stick work was something quite different.

It is not surprising, therefore, that some architectural historians relate this style of 1850-1890 to a much later tradition established by such California architects as Charles and Henry Greene and Bernard Maybeck. This has been styled "structuralism in redwood." Kinship with the Stick Style of the East is evident in the use of braces and brackets, projecting rafters and purlins, and in the attention given to rustically-framed porches and verandas. It seems more logical, however, to consider the Western variation as an extension and adaptation of the Eastern Shingle Style in the manner of the Mission Style. The works of the Greenes in the Los Angeles area, Maybeck in the Bay area, and that of other allied architects is of an overwhelming horizontality that is extremely modern to the contemporary eye. Oriental effects are frequently found in these buildings; Gothic touches are few and far between.

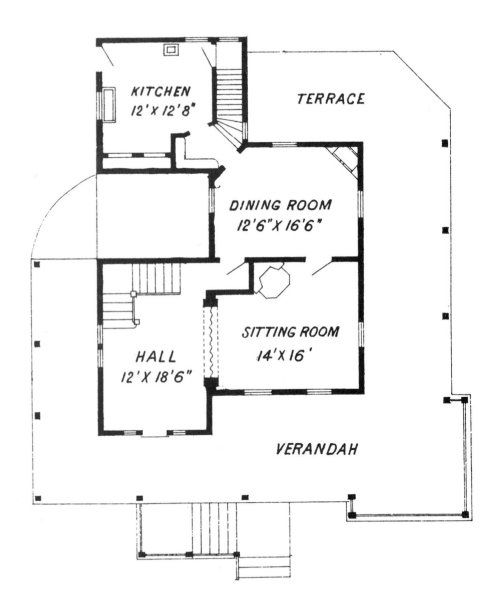

First floor, Seashore house.

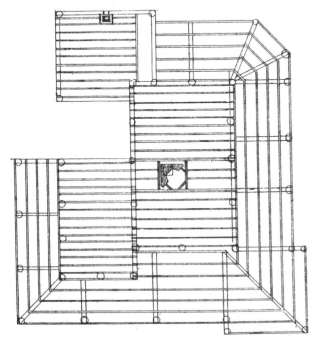

First floor framing plan, Seashore house.

Seashore house, perspective view, William G. Preston, architect, Plate 19, *Modern Architectural Designs and Details* (1881).

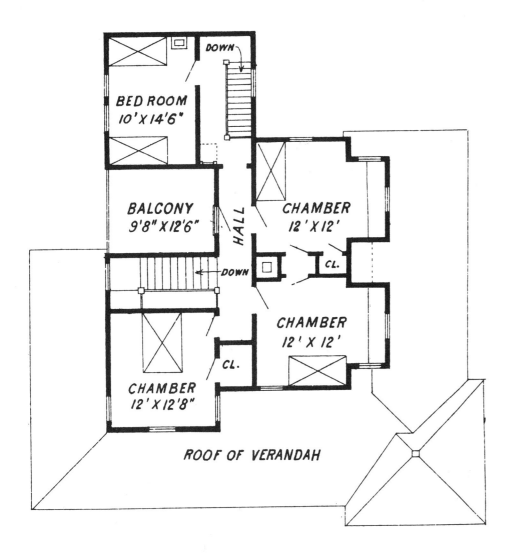

BED ROOM
10' X 14'6"

DOWN

BALCONY
9'8" X 12'6"

HALL

CHAMBER
12' X 12'

DOWN

CL.

CHAMBER
12' X 12'

CL.

CHAMBER
12' X 12'8"

ROOF OF VERANDAH

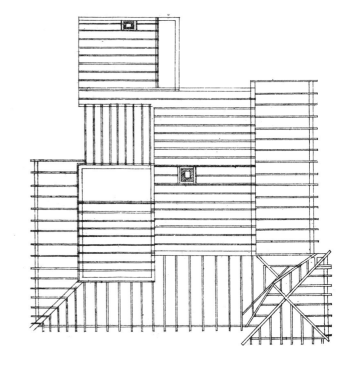

Second story floor and framing plans, Seashore house.

FRONT

EAST SIDE

WEST SIDE

REAR

Framing plans, Seashore house; scale, 1/16″ = 1′.

"Plain Timber Cottage-Villa," Andrew Jackson Downing, Fig. 130 of *The Architecture of Country Houses* (1850). Ornate as this building appears today, it is of the picturesque but structurally honest sort endorsed by Downing and his contemporaries. The relatively simple lines which follow those of the structure itself can be found in many Queen Anne buildings. Increasingly, however, these were overwhelmed by a confusing mixture of materials and ornamentation.

The Queen Anne Style

With the exception of Colonial, the Queen Anne is the most readily recognizable style in North America. It is a term practically synonymous with "Victorian." The multifaceted façades of such buildings are so striking that it is impossible to ignore them wherever they are found—in San Francisco, notably, or in Boston, or in Keokuk, Iowa. To define this style, however, is a more difficult exercise. "Queen Anne" is a term which, in the words of an 1883 critic, "has been made to cover a multitude of incongruities, including indeed, the bulk of recent work which otherwise defies classification, and there is a convenient vagueness about the term which fits it to that use." Ever since the Philadelphia Centennial Exposition of 1876, where half-timbered designs were executed by the British government, home builders and architects seized whatever elements of the style, launched by Richard Norman Shaw in England in 1868, struck their particular fancy. The earliest designs were inspired by Elizabethan forms, but these were gradually subsumed in a novel mixture of the Second Empire or Mansard, Shingle, and Stick styles.

The terminology of the 1880s is no less confusing. Contemporary books of house plans speak of Queen Anne, Elizabethan, and Eastlake styles. Modern day critics continue along the same vein, some substituting the jarring neologism "Jacobethan" for the Elizabethan and Jacobean, but retaining Queen Anne and Eastlake. Distinctions *can* be made between the three modes, and an attempt at doing so is tried here, but for all intents and purposes the term "Queen Anne" can be employed to cover a multitude of architectural virtues and sins. "Elizabethan" or "Jacobethan" refer to parapeted roofs, towers and turrets, and pseudo strapwork ornamentation. "Eastlake" refers to the lavish use of machine-turned architectural elements such as balusters and posts. These are seen most clearly on houses built in the San Francisco area during the 1880s and '90s. English architect Charles Eastlake, the author of *Hints on Household Taste* (first American edition, 1872), was astounded to discover in the 1880s that his designs for domestic furniture had been appropriated for architectural millwork. Many of the structural elements do give the appearance of being turned on a lathe in the same manner as tables and chair legs. In general form, however, "Eastlake" houses do not differ from the Queen Anne. In fact, a recent guide to building styles and terms, *Identifying American Architecture* by John J.-G. Blumenson, uses pictures of the same houses to identify both styles.

What then is a Queen Anne house? It is foremost a strongly asymmetrical building with steep gables, high chimneys, and a rich mixture of construction materials—wood, brick, and sometimes terra cotta, stone, and shingling. Attic and second-story gables often project well beyond lower floors. A tower or turret may be tucked into the side. Iron finials and cresting may appear at critical peaks. As in the Stick Style, porches and verandas sweep around several sides of the building.

The Short Hills, New Jersey, house designed by the New York architectural firm of Lamb & Wheeler in the early 1880s displays many of the above features. The exterior walls are richly ornamented with terra-cotta panels and wood shingling of the fish-scale variety, and lower surfaces are finished with wood clapboarding. The most distinctive element is the turreted oriel which appears almost to be hinged at the corner. The house features "triplet" windows in the parlor and in the oriel. Verandas and a porch extend around three sides of the dwelling. Chimneys are massive and capped in a decoratively flared fashion.

The interior decoration, as shown here, matches the exterior in style. The floor plans faithfully follow the cross-gabled form of the outside. The first-floor rooms are generous spaces, the dining room being slightly larger than the parlor. The former is surely the most gracious room with an opening to a back veranda and, presumably, landscaped grounds.

The second Queen Anne home, an 1883 design from the pages of the *American Agriculturist*, is somewhat smaller in scale, but no less extravagant. The slate roofs laid in belts and crested with ornamental iron along the main ridges first attract the eye. As in the Short Hills house, shingling—this time of redwood—and clapboard siding are combined. Here, however, string courses are used to define the various levels and materials structurally.

The interior of this dwelling displays another significant feature—the elimination of a reception hall and a greatly reduced vestibule. According to the description, "The general arrangement was suggested by a woman who determined to dispense with the conventional main hall and stairway occupying the most prominent place in the front part of the house, providing instead a vestibule entrance

"House at Short Hills, New Jersey," perspective view, Lamb and Wheeler, architects, New York, in *Modern Architectural Designs and Details* (1881).

outside the house from a part of the veranda. This puts the stairs in a less conspicuous place with approaches from two directions at the foot, thus making them serve equally well for general or family use from the main house and as a private stairs from the rear extension." For a family less concerned with appearances and a more modest budget for help, this was a decided improvement.

The windows are quite typical of those found in Queen Anne homes, with single lights of clear glass in the lower sash and several smaller tinted lights in the top portion. "The tinted glass, in a variety of colors," according to the description, "produces, with little cost, a very cheerful effect, both outside and inside." Throughout the interior, woodwork is of pine. Sliding or pocket doors are used to separate the dining and sitting rooms or to open them up at will. The parlor is the most pleasant room in the house, with a large fireplace and four windows opening up to a wide veranda. This room, as well as the other principal first floor rooms, was ornamented with cornices of stucco.

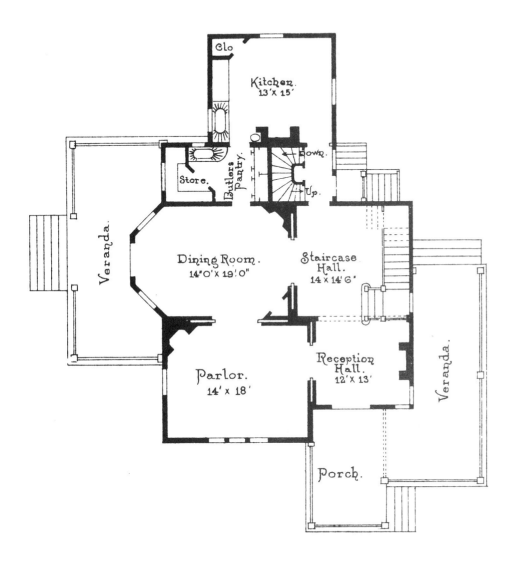

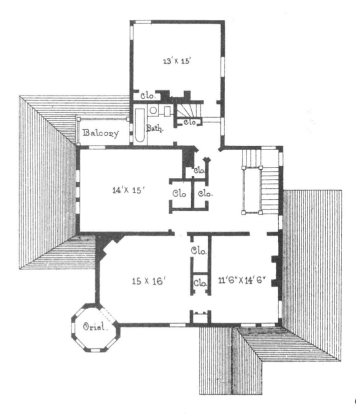

Left and *right*, first and second stories, "House at Short Hills, New Jersey."

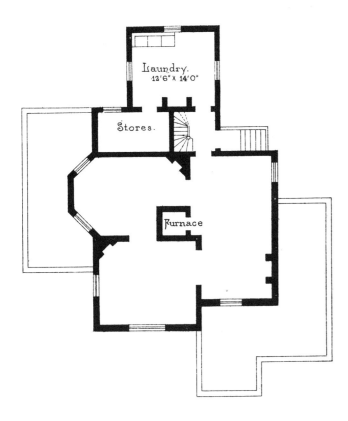

Above and *below*, cellar and attic floor plans, "House at Short Hills."

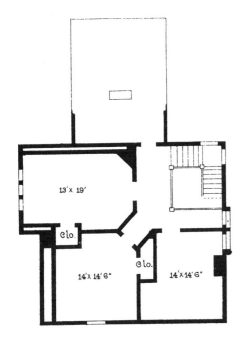

Triplet window and window section through sill, "House at Short Hills."

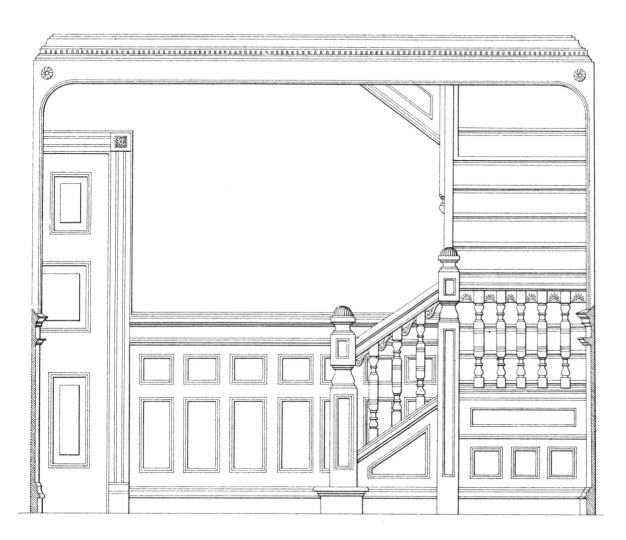

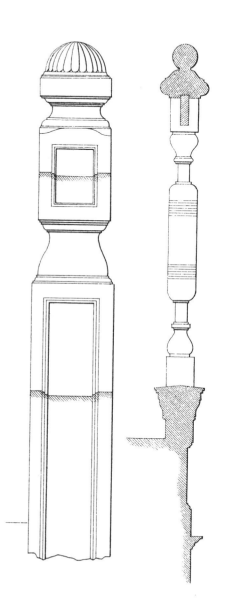

Hall interior, newel, and baluster rail, "House at Short Hills."

"House Costing $2,500," front elevation, *American Agriculturist* (1883).

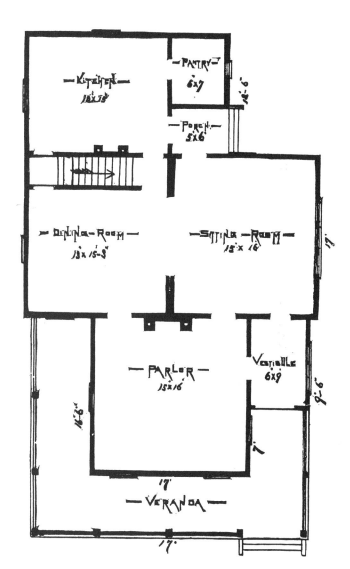

Side elevation and main floor, "House Costing $2,500."

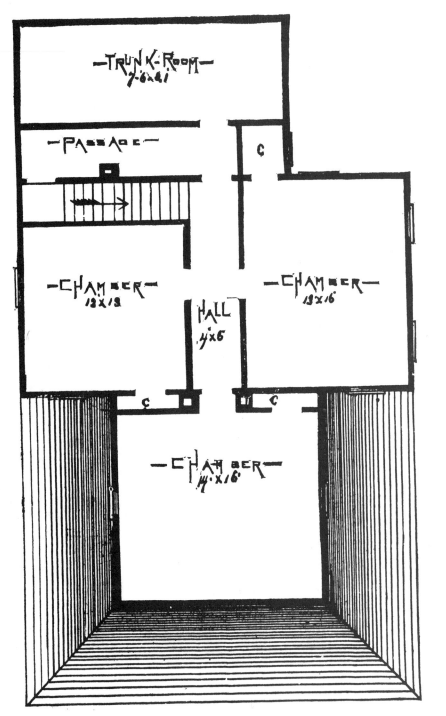

TRUNK-ROOM
7'-6"×41'

PASSAGE

CHAMBER
13×13

HALL
4'×5'

c

CHAMBER
13×16

c c

CHAMBER
14'×16'

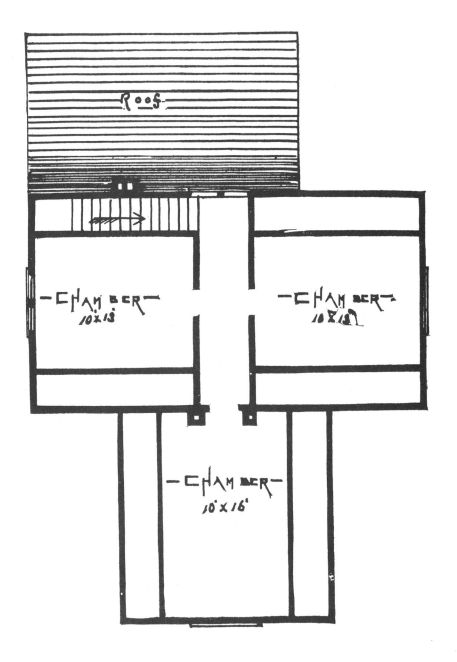

ROOF

CHAMBER
10×13

CHAMBER
10×12

CHAMBER
10'×16'

Left and *right,* second story and attic, ''House Costing $2,500.''

"House at Fairmount, New Jersey," perspective view, Rossiter and Wright, architects, New York, Plate 65, *Modern Architectural Designs and Details* (1881).

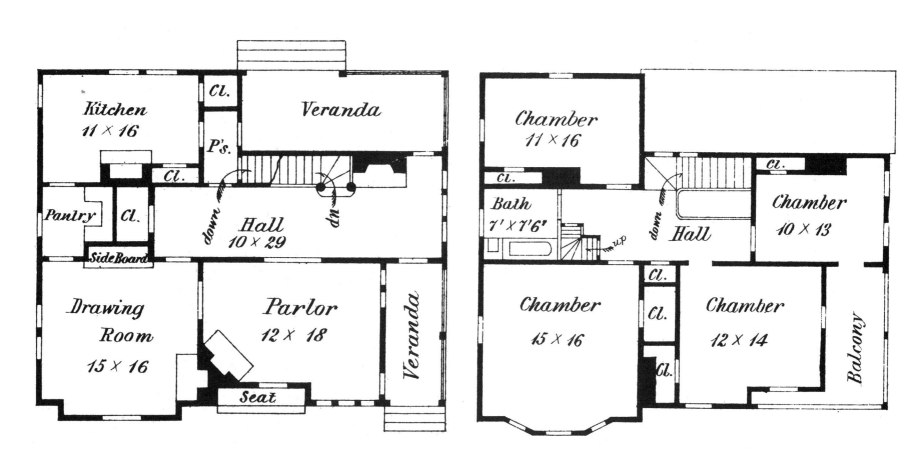

Left and *right*, first and second stories, "House at Fairmount."

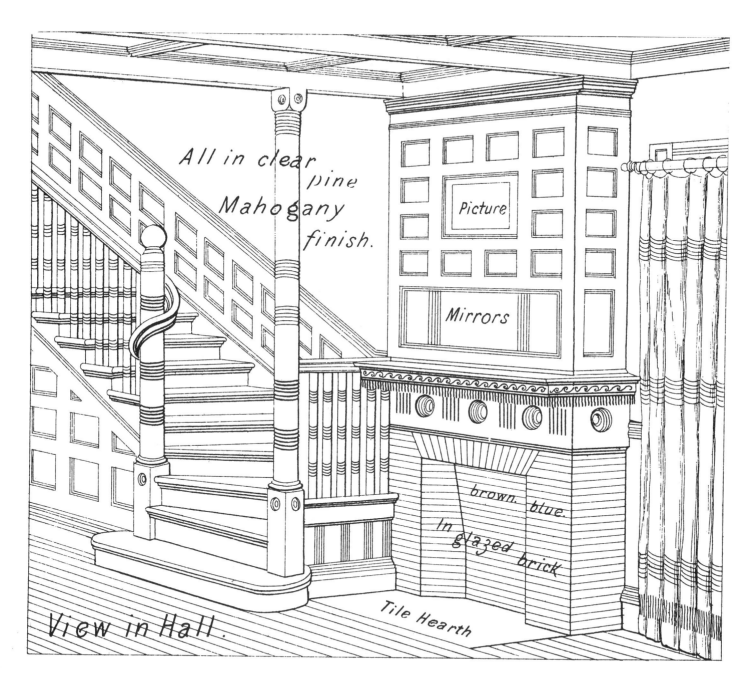

All in clear pine Mahogany finish.

Picture

Mirrors

View in Hall.

brown. blue.

In glazed brick

Tile Hearth

Hall view and details, "House at Fairmount."

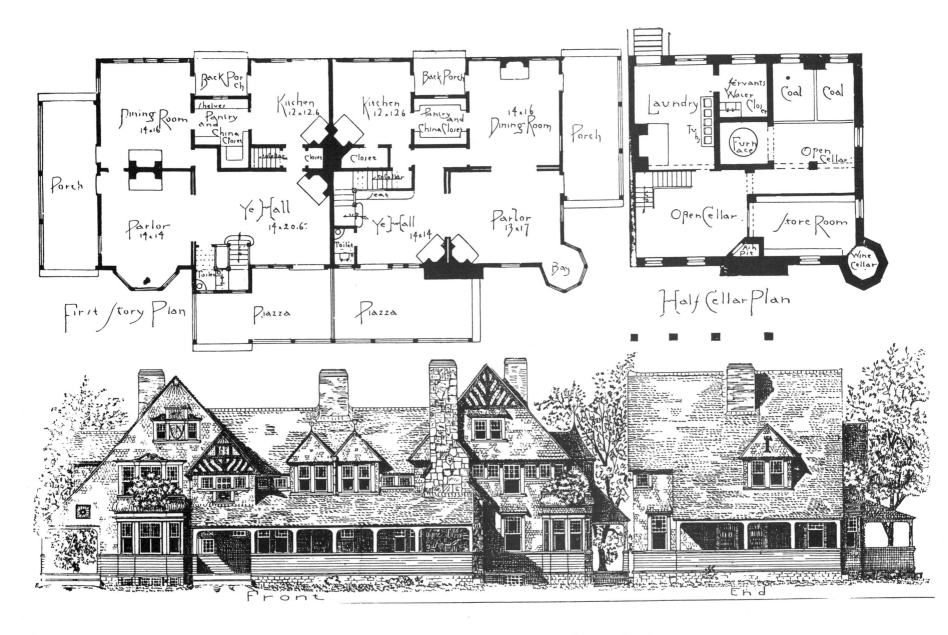

Double house, Design 159 in *Palliser's New Cottage Homes* (1887). The Elizabethan half-timbered style emerged with more and more strength in the late 1880s and '90s, and typical Queen Anne "gingerbread" was replaced with large amounts of shingling or coarse stone work.

Country house, Bertram Grosvenor Goodhue, architect, *Architecture and Building* (1891). Goodhue was an extraordinarily versatile architect and at this time was working for the firm of Renwick, Aspinwall & Russell in New York. He is best known today for his work in the Spanish Colonial and Beaux Arts styles.

The Shingle Style

Well-to-do Americans of the late nineteenth century, increasingly successful in the affairs of the industrial marketplace, sought comfortable, fashionable dwelling places worthy of their new prosperity. Smaller homes closer to growing center cities were abandoned for green suburban estates. Truly successful men of business could afford to build yet a second new house, a vacation retreat for their families along an unspoiled coastal area or amidst mountain greenery. At first the new homes—suburban or vacation—were baronial in style, imitating the Stick Style or deriving from the Jacobean-style country houses popularized by Richard Norman Shaw and other British architects in the 1870s. By the 1880s, however, a more American form—the Shingle Style—was emerging.

As in so many matters of American architectural style, Henry Hobson Richardson was preeminent as a spokesman. The vertical thrust of the Stick Style and the Jacobean gave way in his plans to much greater horizontality. Wood paneling and half-timber construction was replaced on exterior surfaces with horizontal shingling. Certain elements of a seventeenth-century Colonial American style came into reuse—the gambrel roof; simple building materials such as wood shingles, a snug, close-to-the-earth profile. Americans had rediscovered their colonial heritage in the decade following the Centennial celebration, and while they still aped English manners, the leaders in style were receptive to the new architectural aesthetic. As numerous historians have explained, it was the beginning of a new era in building.

The elements of the style are unmistakable, and very much in evidence in the home built for H. K. Wilcox in Middletown, New York, by a Richardsonian disciple, E. G. W. Dietrich. Here is found a blending of Colonial Revival and Romanesque forms as well as reminders of the past Gothic tradition. The broadly shaped gambrel roof of the center portion of the house flows down and is anchored on a stone Romanesque base. This vast expanse of roof is broken with a fanlight and a row of shuttered, double-sash windows, and overhangs an arched entryway and a single bay window. On the side of the house, a massive chimney has been tucked into the sloping angle of the central gambrel; aside it is a second gambrel broken by a Palladian window, a double bay, and a single bay window. As if to pay proper respect to the Gothic Revival past, a lancet window appears in the front façade (in a room designated as the "library"). The bay windows and diamond-shaped panes in some of the sashes are further evidence of a lingering nostalgia for Gothic taste.

As eclectic as it is, the overall conception and composition of the Dietrich-designed house is Richardsonian and in the Shingle Style. The angles of the gambrels define the structure in every respect, sweeping down to include the side and back porches. Gambrels and porches, as Vincent Scully has written concerning the work of a similar architect, are interwoven "in a direct expression of continuity between interior and exterior spaces." The first and second floor plans testify to that basic plan.

From the massive Romanesque entryway one enters a vestibule and grand reception hall. This central space, with its monumental staircase as the focus, provides an entryway to all rooms of the house and largely determines their function. Prominently positioned on the front side of the house are the parlor, with working fireplace, and library with a massive hearth and bay window seats. Immediately behind these two areas are slightly less important rooms: a den with fireplace and, on the other side of the center hall, the dining room which opens up to the butler's pantry, and thus to the kitchen. A small conservatory is attached to a corner of the dining area. The architect has also allowed for movement between the dining area and the library, an agreeable arrangement for gentlemen wishing to retire from table to easy chair. Service areas of the house are properly positioned at the back of the house—butler's pantry, kitchen, cold storage area, pantry storage, and work room.

The second floor sleeping areas further testify to the elevated living style of the Wilcox family. The bedrooms are supplied with large storage closets and are well-lighted comfortable rooms, three of which are equipped with fireplaces. The master bedroom to the right is a particularly handsome area with a nook and window seats providing a private, cosy retreat. Again, as on the first floor, service rooms are positioned at the back—a servant's bedroom, and linen closets.

Homes built in the Shingle Style made room for not only functional spaces but graceful, inviting areas—a conservatory for greenery; bay window nooks with built-in window seats for quiet moments; an open, center reception hall for the display of sculpture and other artwork; sweeping, curved porches for summer relaxation. This was a gilded age for those who could afford to enjoy it in high style.

H. K. Wilcox residence, Middletown, New York, 1891,
E. G. W. Dietrich, architect

Second floor

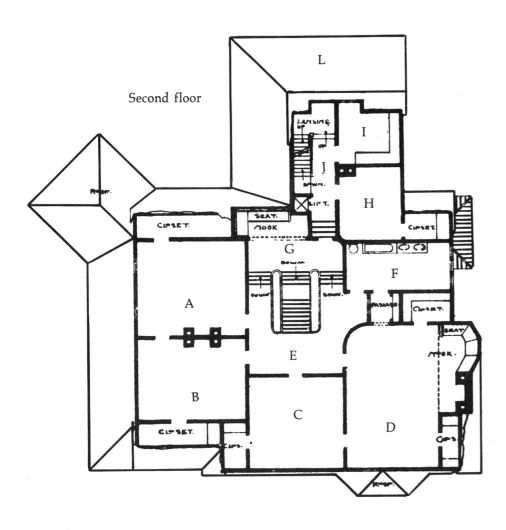

First floor, Wilcox residence: *A* parlor, 14 × 15.9; *B* reception hall, 16 × 20; *C,G* vestibule; *D* library, 14 × 20.10; *E* dining room, 17 × 22; *F* den, 14 × 12; *H* butler's pantry; *I* conservatory; *J* workroom, 8 × 16; *K* kitchen, 14.6 × 16; *L* refrigerator

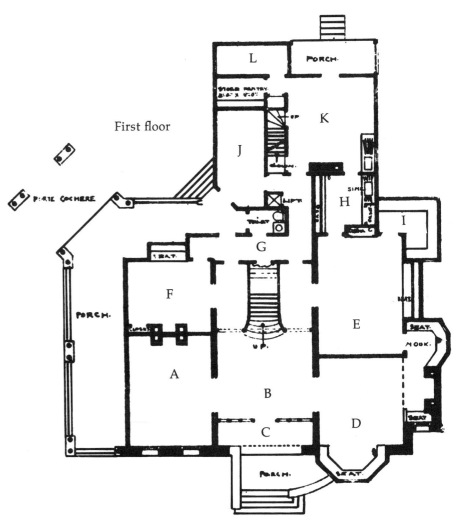

First floor

Second floor, Wilcox residence; *A,B,C,D* bedroom, *E* hall, *F* bathroom, *G* landing, *H* servant's room, *I* linen closets, *J* back hall and landing, *K,L* porch.

From the massive Romanesque entryway one enters a vestibule and grand reception hall. This central space, with its monumental staircase as the focus, provides an entryway to all rooms of the house and largely determines their function. Prominently positioned on the front side of the house are the parlor, with working fireplace, and library with a massive hearth and bay window seats. Immediately behind these two areas are slightly less important rooms: a den with fireplace and, on the other side of the center hall, the dining room which opens up to the butler's pantry, and thus to the kitchen. A small conservatory is attached to a corner of the dining area. The architect has also allowed for movement between the dining area and the library, an agreeable arrangement for gentlemen wishing to retire from table to easy chair. Service areas of the house are properly positioned at the back of the house—butler's pantry, kitchen, cold storage area, pantry storage, and work room.

The second floor sleeping areas further testify to the elevated living style of the Wilcox family. The bedrooms are supplied with large storage closets and are well-lighted comfortable rooms, three of which are equipped with fireplaces. The master bedroom to the right is a particularly handsome area with a nook and window seats providing a private, cosy retreat. Again, as on the first floor, service rooms are positioned at the back—a servant's bedroom, and linen closets.

Homes built in the Shingle Style made room for not only functional spaces but graceful, inviting areas—a conservatory for greenery; bay window nooks with built-in window seats for quiet moments; an open, center reception hall for the display of sculpture and other artwork; sweeping, curved porches for summer relaxation. This was a gilded age for those who could afford to enjoy it in high style.

Cottage, Design 168 in *Palliser's New Cottage Homes* (1887). The cost was estimated at $2,300.

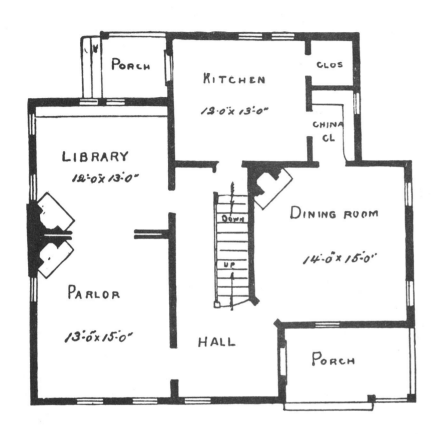

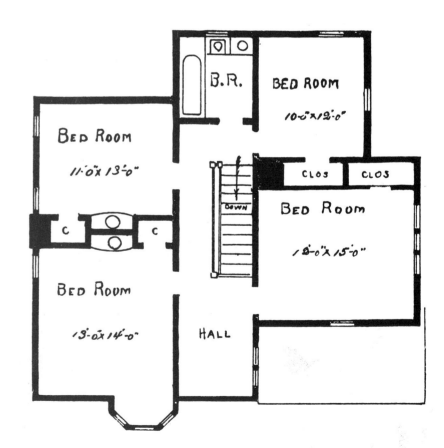

First and second floors, cottage.

DEXTER BROS.' ENGLISH SHINGLE STAIN.

This House is Stained with Dexter Bros.' English Shingle Stain.

RESIDENCE OF THOMAS LORD, EVANSTON, ILL.
Burnham & Root, Architects, Chicago.

"WE CHALLENGE ANYONE TO SHOW US A HOUSE WHERE OUR STAIN HAS WASHED OFF."

Advertisement featuring the residence of Thomas Lord designed by the famed Chicago architectural firm, Burnham and Root. From *Architecture and Building* (1893). Here the Queen Anne Style residence has been almost completely shingled over. A natural, stained finish such as this was favored then for its easy maintenance and warm quality.

81

"House in North Park," E. G. W. Dietrich, architect, New York. From *Architecture and Building* (1898).

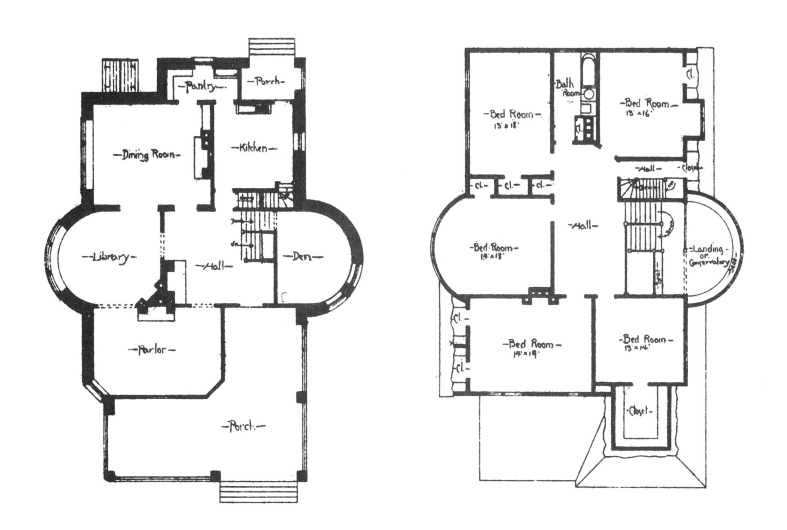

First and second floors, "House in North Park."

"House at Sheepshead Bay, Long Island," Fowler and Hough,
architects, New York. From *Architecture and Building* (1897).

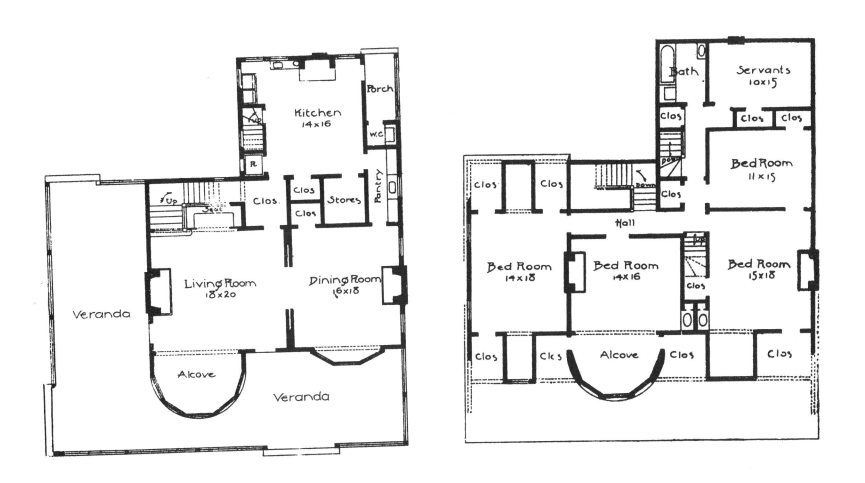

First and second floors, "House at Sheepshead
Bay."

The Romanesque Style

Romanesque forms are important component elements in the visual vocabulary of North American architecture. The semicircular arch was introduced during the 1840s in entrances and windows and persisted in use throughout the century under various stylistic guises—Romanesque Revival, Victorian Romanesque, and Richardsonian Romanesque. In addition to the arch, many brick and/or stone buildings featured such structural forms as the rounded buttress, curvilinear wall, and tower. The overall profile was often massive and was suited perfectly to such structures as churches, governmental offices, schools, and railroad stations. The Romanesque did not become a popular style for home building until the 1880s and '90s. Its great master and popularizer, Henry Hobson Richardson, died in 1886, and in his wake the architectural community strove to introduce the style in every possible way.

Many of the earliest buildings and all those of Richardson himself are relatively restrained in decoration and present a monochromatic masonry façade. Richardson's structures are unique in their utter dependence on mass and scale for their impact. The Glessner House in Chicago (1885), one of the masterpieces of American domestic architecture, depends for its character only on the placement of quarry-faced stone blocks and their relation to entryway arches, window openings, and a low roof line. Through the massing of shapes in an almost sculptured fashion, something truly original was created out of stone. The firm of Burnham and Root was equally successful in its interpretations of the Romanesque in such structures as The Rookery (1886) and the Ayer House (1885), both in Chicago.

The Romanesque, as applied to domestic architecture, was usually treated in a more ornamental manner, and such homes constitute by far a majority of buildings in this style. Exterior masonry walls were frequently rendered more decorative through the use of various colored and textured stone in bands, trim, and arches. This created a polychromatic effect which was picturesque, yet in keeping with a fortress-like appearance. Brick and terra-cotta tiles or panels were also used to emphasize and embellish structural elements such as windows, roof lines, gables, and entryways. This was the *Victorian* Romanesque, a vernacular style that balanced the ornamental with the functional, the verical thrust of Gothic with the horizontal emphasis of the arch.

Such a balance is reflected in the James J. Wait residence in Chicago, designed by Dwight Heald Perkins at the turn of the century. Brick forms the exterior walls and is used to define the first from the second floors in a belt course and in what is called a corbel table just below the course of dentils, also in brick. This is most visible in the side view seen here. Stone has been employed for the lintels, and terra-cotta decoration appears to punctuate the brick belt course.

Windows are not simply arched but are shaped in a somewhat Moorish fashion that is in keeping with the Spanish Romanesque tradition. This is a town house and one obviously designed for a fairly narrow lot. From the side, the full mass of the structure becomes visible. The porch, which assumes so much prominence from the street, is thrown back into relief. Use of heavy square pillars, decorated only at the top, ties the addition to the massive structure lying behind it. Directly above the porch is a bay window which owes more in style to the Gothic than to the Romanesque. The roof tiles on this bay, however, help to relate it to the porch and main structure which are also roofed in tile.

The interior of the dwelling is similar to that found in many town houses of the time. The main entrance is on the side and is not reached from the porch. A spacious entry hall has been provided in the center of the house and this allows for direct passage to one principal room or another. The monotonous floor plan of so many city dwellings built on a restricted and expensive site, with one room linked to another in "railroad flat" fashion, has thus been avoided. The rooms on the first and second floors vary in shape, and communication between the floors is arranged functionally from either the front hall or the service area which comprises the "butler's pantry."

The second house illustrated here, a city dwelling designed in 1891 by C. D. Marvin of New York, more closely approximates the Romanesque Rivival "ideal." The basic form is not unlike that encountered in the first building—a masonry block in the middle of which a projecting gable section is positioned. This building also presents a narrow profile from the street. The main entrance and the windows of the first floor, however, are strictly arched in coarsed stone voussoirs. This stone provides a stylish contrast to the general brickwork. Both the main arch, and the secondary opening next to it on the side, end in columned piers, a common element in the Romanesque. It is difficult to ascertain whether the decorative cornice work is executed in stone or in terra cotta, but, in either case, this sort of

decorative detail is a familiar touch.

Floor plans for this residence are not available. The interior would have provided for a large reception hall containing the central staircase. The front room at left probably served as living room or parlor; and that behind the large arched window at the side, as the dining room.

Romanesque Style buildings of this sort have been a favorite target of the wrecker's ball in recent years. Their very monumentality seems to challenge destruction. Such stone- or brickwork buildings, of course, cannot be cosmetically treated quite as easily with paint as can frame structures. And given the quality of today's air, it is remarkable that the stonework of many such urban buildings has resisted severe corrosion. Consequently, such homes often present a bedraggled, down-at-the-heels appearance. Romanesque buildings have another strike against them—they often appear cold and forbidding to the modern eye. Although a few may be frightful mammoths best buried with the other bones of the past, the majority are surely much more imaginative and inviting domestic dwelling places than their modern jerry-built counterparts.

Design for a town residence, A. Beatty Orth, architect, 1896.

James J. Wait residence, front view, Chicago,
Dwight Heald Perkins, architect, Chicago.
From *The Western Architect* (1903).

Side view, Wait residence.

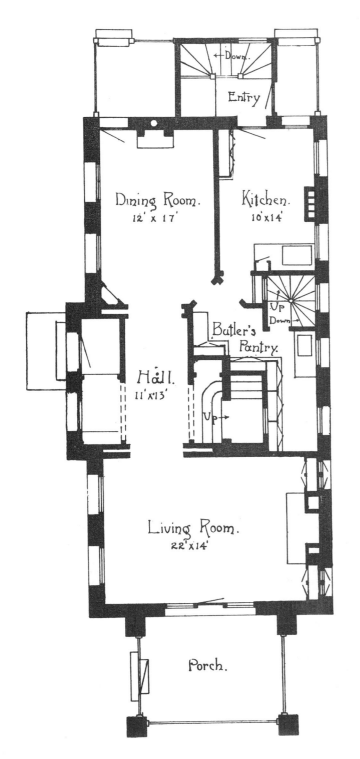

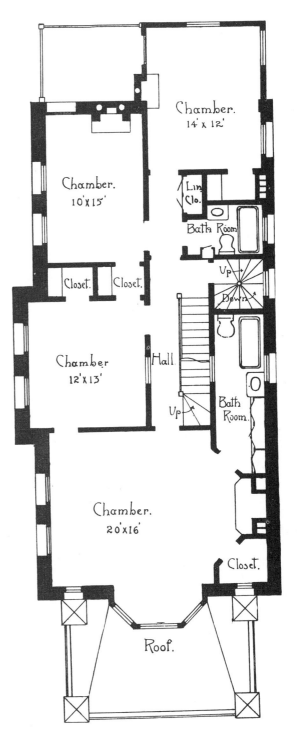

First and second stories, Wait residence.

"Design for a City House," C. D. Marvin, architect, New York. From *Architecture and Building* (1891).

John Mathews residence, New York,
Lamb and Rich, architects, 1897.

The English Tudor Style

Nostalgia for the 1920s, the last period before the trauma of Depression, is widely expressed and indulged today. The building styles of the period, however, are just being re-examined. In terms of architecture, the time was a "snobbish" one, and the English style has been rightly termed "Stockbroker's Tudor" by one critic. In a vainglorious search for proper antecedents, wealthy Americans of British descent not only sought to establish genealogical links with their Colonial and Waspish past, but aped the manners and copied the manor house style of days gone by. Entire English manor houses were brought to America and reconstructed with infinite care and expense. Various kinds of architectural ornamentation and structural elements, of course, were ripped away from their European roots with the signing of sufficiently large checks. The Gatsbys of the time, although unable to establish a right to join the Sons of the American Revolution or the Order of St. George, fell right in with the antiquarian spirit.

Wealthy Americans turned to several building forms for their dream houses. The massive, half-timbered manor of the Jacobean sort, with gate house, stable, and other dependencies, was one suitable prototype. Architect Richard Norman Shaw had interpreted this form in the English countryside and in London's Bedford Park neighborhood during the 1860s and '70s, and Henry Hobson Richardson followed in somewhat the same direction for a period of time in America with considerable originality. Richardson moved on to articulate the Shingle Style; lesser talents interpreted the English heritage in more conventional ways. The style was known as "Elizabethan" at the time, and was, in fact, a variant of the Queen Anne. By the 1920s, what had been called "Elizabethan" had disappeared from view along with the Queen Anne style of building. The new English Tudor was a more "correct" form in that it imitated an historical style with greater fidelity. Fortunately, however, the best architects at work in the Tudor genre were not slavish to the past, and few devoted their time exclusively to sprawling country estates.

More modest in size than the manor house was the stone Cotswold cottage. Considerably larger than the term suggests to Americans, it was, nonetheless, scaled down not only in size but in the extent of its ornamentation. Suburban areas of Philadelphia, especially the Chestnut Hill section, are composed of homes directly inspired by the humbler tradition of Cotswold masonry construction. Harold Donaldson Eberlein, an estimable critic and historian of American architecture in the early decades of this century, thought the Cotswold form an ideal one for suburban houses, and argued that, "To revert to the Cotswold type of architecture for present inspiration in domestic design . . . is neither . . . a bit of affectation and archaeological pedantry, nor a piece of Anglo maniac inanity. It is only asserting our indefeasible right to a lawful part of our national heritage." Eberlein was, of course, projecting his own social prejudices and those of the class he served. Nevertheless, a close look at the stone homes of Chestnut Hill that he was defending leads one to the conclusion that he was right—for whatever reason. Again, in his own words, "No attempt was made to *reproduce* any Cotswold house, or group of houses; that would have been foolish. But by drawing inspiration from Cotswold models for the general manner of treatment and by making such adaptations as the needs of the individual case dictated, a result was achieved wholly satisfactory to all concerned—including the occupants, harmonious with the natural environment, and consistent in the employment of materials native to the locality. What more could any one desire?"

Now that English Tudor is taking its place along with the Colonial Revival in the pantheon of officially recognized historical styles, there is little reason for questioning its *raison d'etre*. What remains is the detailed examination of the elements which define the style and provide a means for its evaluation. This is no simple matter. "English" Tudor houses are decidedly North American—just as the Georgian Colonial and Italianate were naturalized—and combine in varying degrees elements of Norman, Elizabethan, and Jacobean styles. Some houses are overwhelmingly severe or Romanesque in profile, and others display the full richness of the late Tudor style—strapwork, parapets, projecting bays. The most commonly encountered exterior feature is that of half-timbering. The timbers used in "The Close," a Short Hills, New Jersey, residence designed by the architectural firm of Soldwedel and Tatton, illustrated here, are of chestnut framed and pinned together. The space between them is filled with brick and has been stuccoed. The sharply pitched roof is of the hip variety and is broken by projecting cross gables. Windows are casement and contain leaded glass. The bay windows are typical of English Tudor and may, as noted in the courtyard photograph, extend two floors. The basic

"The Close," Short Hills, New Jersey, Soldwedel and Tatton, architects, c. 1920.

plan is "L"-shaped and provides for an attractive arrangement of the rooms off a courtyard.

The most distinctive interior spaces of "The Close" are the three rooms in the main block—reception hall, dining room, and living room. The same rustic appearance is effected in the interior by the use of massive fireplaces in the living and dining rooms, exposed wood beams and intricately formed plaster strapwork in the ceiling, paneled wainscoting, a musicians gallery, and the nooks formed by the bays.

Several special features of "The Close" are its red terra cotta tile roof and the provision for a long gallery or passage on both the first and second floors overlooking the courtyard. The average North American Tudor residence is much more likely to have a slate roof and to display an impressive chimney topped with at least several courses of brick and terra cotta pots. More ambitious home owners carried the period detailing much further with the addition of such exterior features as carved stone ornaments, cast terra-cotta forms, casement and oriel windows, parapets, and battlements.

Every metropolitan area in North America contains its neighborhood of English Tudor homes—large and small. Some of these feature eaves sweeping almost to the ground, providing an arched shelter for an entryway or garage. This particular form suggests the influence of Richardson and his followers in the early Queen Anne and in the Shingle styles. The overall perspective is one of overwhelming horizontality, a tying of the structure to its site. This appreciation of the natural environment is also expressed by the use of fine building materials in grand and modest homes—good hardwoods, fieldstone, terra cotta, copper and zinc, leaded glass, cast and wrought iron. The craftsmanship and quality of materials displayed in many such homes now located in declining neighborhoods make them especially attractive real estate investments. Only their spacious dimensions pose problems for the energy-conscious owner.

Main entrance, "The Close."

Courtyard with view of inside opening of covered entryway,
"The Close."

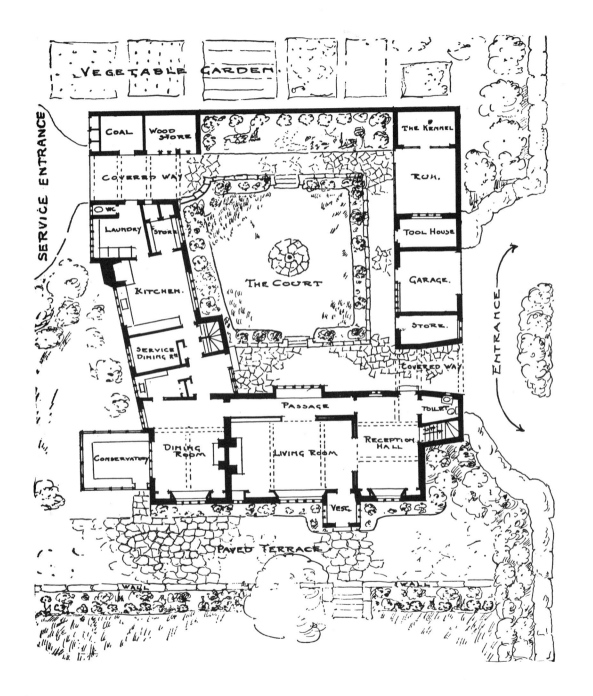

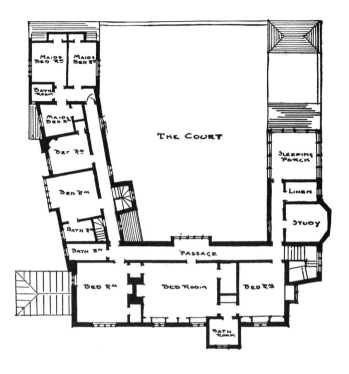

First and second floors, "The Close."

VEGETABLE GARDEN

SERVICE ENTRANCE

COAL | WOOD STORE

COVERED WAY

WC

LAUNDRY | STORE

KITCHEN.

SERVICE DINING R?

CONSERVATORY

DINING ROOM

LIVING ROOM

RECEPTION HALL

VEST.

PASSAGE

TOILET

PAVED TERRACE

WALL | WALL

THE COURT

THE KENNEL

RUN.

TOOL HOUSE

GARAGE.

STORE.

COVERED WAY

ENTRANCE

THE COURT

MAIDS BED R? | MAIDS BED R?

BATH ROOM

MAIDS BED R?

BED R?

BED RM

BATH R?

BATH RM

BED RM | BED ROOM | BED R?

PASSAGE

BATH ROOM

SLEEPING PORCH

LINEN

STUDY

PLASTER OR CEMENT CEILING

"Dwelling in the Elizabethan Style," Front (*left*) and side (*right*) elevations, Plate 76 in *Architectural Designs and Details* (1881). Elizabethan, Queen Anne, Jacobethan—whatever you wish to call it—found its fullest expression in the Tudor Revival period. Thirty years earlier it was an eclectic motif that competed with others.

Porch   Conservatory

Porch   Butler   DINING ROOM   SITTING ROOM

                        PARLOR   HALL

STABLE   KITCHEN   HALL   up   LIBRARY

                                              Porch

        Vest.

FIRST FLOOR

House keeper   CHAMBER   CHAMBER   Dressing Room   NURSERY   ENTRY

            Bath   Cl   Cl   Cl

STABLE   REAR HALL   HALL

            Linen Room   down   SEWING ROOM   CHAMBER   Dressing Room

SECOND FLOOR

100

"English Cottage," c. 1925. Shingling remained in the gable and the long sloping roof, but the stucco finish and stone trim emphasized the essential Tudor Revival masonry composition. This home was termed an "Elizabethan for Today."

Opposite, proposed residence, John M. Briggs, Cedarhurst, Long Island, 1890.

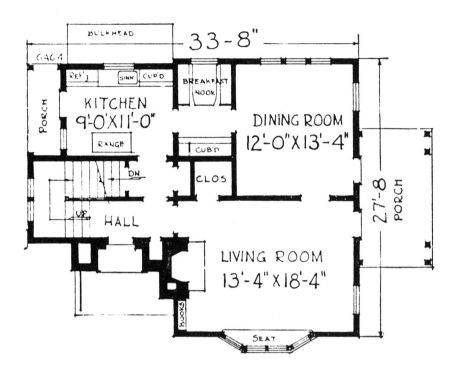

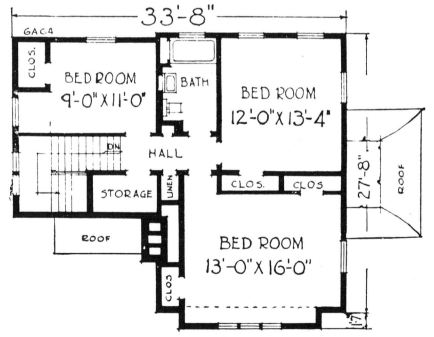

First and second floors, "English Cottage."

Details of a brick, stucco, and half-timbered residence, mid-1920s.

The Spanish Colonial Revival Style

Residents of America's East Coast frequently need reminding that a second and parallel tradition to English Colonial exists in the Spanish Colonial or Mission styles. This is especially ironic considering the fact that many thousands of so-called "Spanish Colonial" homes were built in the residential areas of the East during the early twentieth century. In fact, imitating the Hispanic spirit in building was as much a national craze of the 1920s as the game of mah-jongg. Suitable models—mission churches, ranch houses, forts in a Mexican baroque tradition—existed long before the West and Southwest were anglicized. These adobe brick structures are rarely found except in the last settled areas of New Mexico, Arizona, and southern California, but the romantic spirit which suffuses such a best-selling novel as Willa Cather's *Death Comes for the Archbishop* (1927), set amidst the old-world charm of Santa Fe, transcends time and place. Americans have excelled at movie sets and in adapting the past to their present needs for charm and comfort.

Little attention was paid during the revival of Spanish Colonial to the subtleties of the tradition. As in any vernacular rendering, a nonconformist has been at work. The Georgian Style easily slips into the early English Colonial; the Mansard to the Queen Anne; and the Mission to the Spanish Colonial Revival. Historians tell us that the Mission Style thrived from 1890 to 1920 and is recognized by a simplicity of form and lack of surface decoration. Yet, the so-called Spanish Colonial Revival style of 1915-1940, based on the original style of the 1600-1840 period, was often presented in a similar manner. For every example in American architectural history, there is an exception.

Interest in the Spanish Colonial past was first awakened in the West, particularly California, in the last years of the nineteenth century. It was a style well suited for important buildings such as town halls, railroad stations, and, of course, the church. The missions which stretch along the Pacific coast were and are the most obvious reminders of the now-distant and therefore romantic past. A Mission style in the decorative arts was accompanied by the architectural revival. By World War I, the initial impulse of this movement was spent, and in its place soon came a second awakening that was more pointedly directed to the home-building market throughout the country.

Some Spanish Colonial buildings in temperate areas make ample use of one prominent feature of the style—the patio. Floor plans are shaped to draw the resident into this pleasant enclosure. Homes built in the North, of course, are often without this key element. All buildings, however, do share at least a few of the following features—flat or low pitched red- or blue-tiled roofs, arched entryways or arcades, and white stucco or smooth plastered walls. Wrought- or cast-iron window grilles and railings appear on some homes; exterior walls often carry baroque plaster ornamentation.

The ranch estate of Thomas H. Ince in Beverly Hills, California, is one of the most beautiful Spanish Colonial homes of the twentieth century. Ince, a pioneering silent movie actor, producer, and director, commissioned Roy Sheldon Price to design his home, "Dias Dorados," in 1923. "The long, low plaster walls, simple roof lines, arches and natural rock work," according to *The American Architect and The Architectural Review*, "are the very spirit of the Padres. One feels, more than sees, the softening charm of age this group suggests." As the photographs and floor plans indicate, a "group" of buildings it was. The main entrance is reached through an arcaded loggia. Just across the lengthy main hall, linking two almost separate units, is the patio, a section of which is illustrated here. The section on the left contains such secondary rooms as the kitchen, pantries, servants' rooms, and the dining room; the area to the right of the main entrance is devoted principally to a palatial living room and a library. Few of the so-called "Padres" lived in such splendor. According to the magazine, "The house and buildings are all of the most substantial construction and produced by Mexican labor. The various decorative elements of tiles, textiles and ironwork are also of Mexican labor, and the whole achieves a result that carries to the finest completion the traditions of the section." As is evident from the interior shots, considerable care was lavished on appropriate furnishings and fittings. This was Hollywood Babylon at its best.

What saves "Dias Dorados" from the giganticism that afflicts so many large estates is the careful reproduction of traditional elements in a proper scale. The whole is successful because it is made up of a series of buildings. The main entrance section is a low-lying two-story arcade with a long overhanging second-story porch. The rafters supporting the porch and the eaves extend beyond the wall to cast a cool shadow over the arcade.

No small residence can match the splendor of the Ince estate, but the 1928 Spanish Colonial bungalow illustrated here is charming in its modesty and style. "The real Spanish

Ranch estate, Thomas H. Ince, Beverly Hills, California, Roy
Seldon Price, architect, 1923.

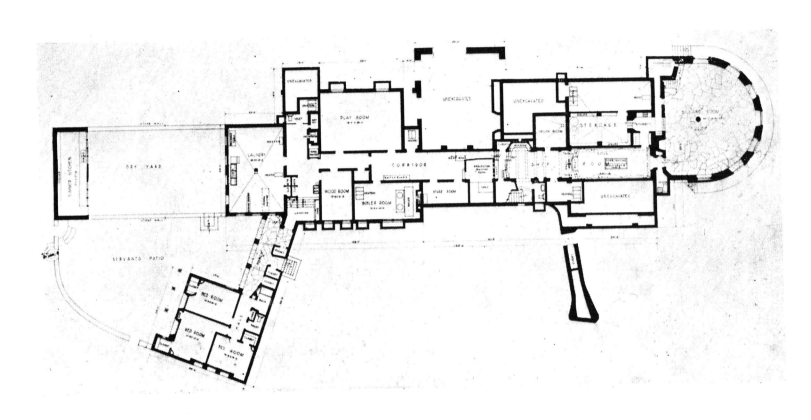

Basement plan, ranch estate.

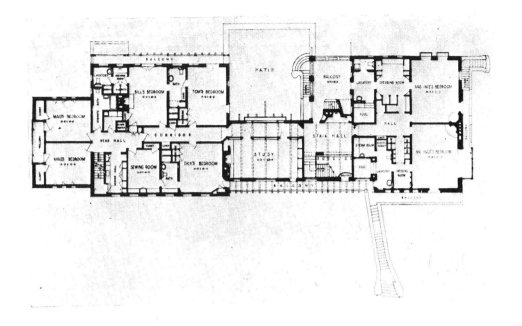

Second and first floors, ranch estate.

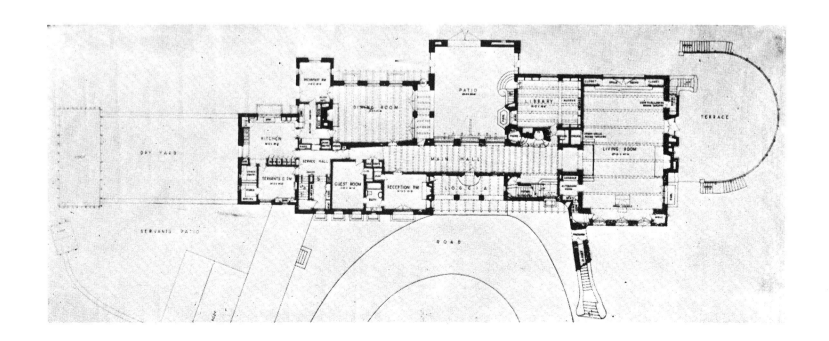

Main entrance and main staircase, ranch estate. The stairwell displays the use of Mexican tiles and wool hangings, and hand-carved beams.

or 'Southern California' style of home, built in any part of the United States today," a '20s critic writes, "must have a patio if it is to be true to form. Even now we find the patio useful in many delightful ways." The positioning of the patio at the front of the bungalow is one of its inspired features. The usual position of this garden area was at the back of the house and away from the noise of the road or street. Here it provides a handsome walled courtyard through which to enter the house.

The positioning of the garage is another unusual feature for the time. In the early days of the automobile, garages were often separated from the house in the same manner that a stable or horse shed was set off from the main dwelling. In this case, the garage is not merely "attached" in an attempt to give the illusion of greater living space, but it functionally forms one side of the patio and aesthetically blends in with the overall design.

The bungalow displays other elements of the revival style which are encountered throughout the country. Doors are of the rustic wood construction favored for interior or exteriors. Ornamental ironwork is used on these and in other spots. The massive chimney is similarly rusticated and is fully exposed against the patio wall and the red tile roof.

The floor plan illustrates an attention to "convenience" which was thoroughly up-to-date and very much of concern to the '20s. Bedrooms are situated just off the main entrance to one side; the living room is only a few steps away across the hall. The kitchen is found at the rear with a dining nook and direct access to the rear bedroom. As in any proper residence of the time, space was allocated for a formal dining room. From the kitchen entry area one could descend to a half-basement which contained laundry, storage, and furnace rooms. A home of the day that was more compact and gracious is hard to visualize.

Homes in the Spanish Colonial tradition have virtually ceased to be built today while the various step-children and orphans of the English Colonial tradition continue to proliferate. This is a distinct loss because the style is well-suited to vast areas of the North American continent and lends itself most readily to modern interpretation. The clean, handsome designs of California architects of the 1920s such as Irving Gill, Wallace Neff, and Bernard Maybeck anticipated the spare structuralism of the International Style but, in the opinion of many, successfully mixed the comfort of a graceful tradition with the demands of modern life for convenience in a way that has never been equalled.

Stairway, ranch estate, leading from second floor balcony to a wading pool and lake "plunge."

109

Patio, ranch estate.

"Spanish Colonial Bungalow," 1928.

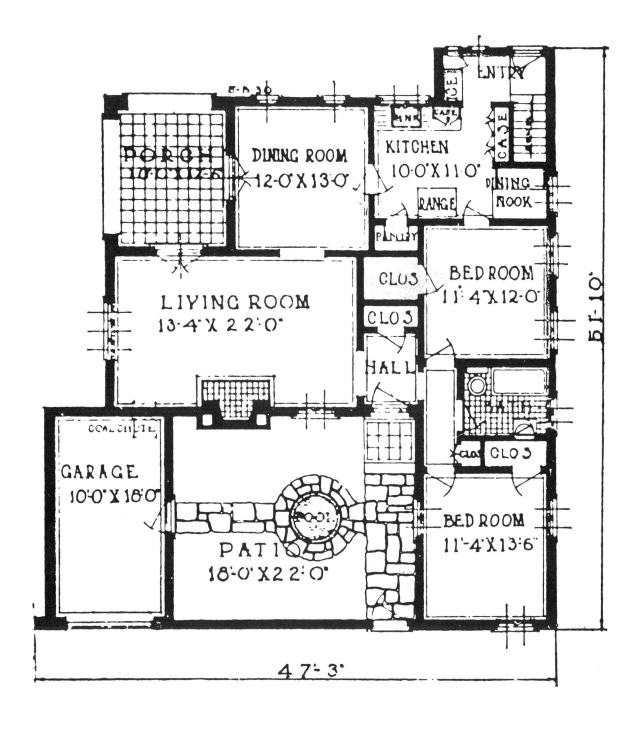

Floor plan, "Spanish Colonial Bungalow."

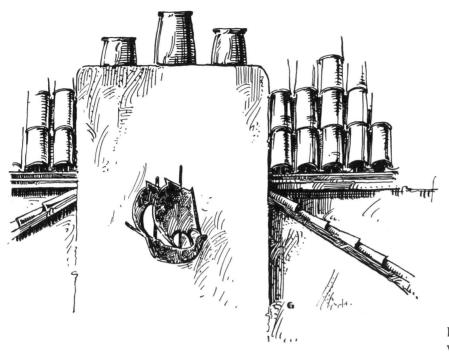

Details characteristic of Spanish Colonial Revival homes built in the early twentieth century.

"Spanish Bungalow," 1928.

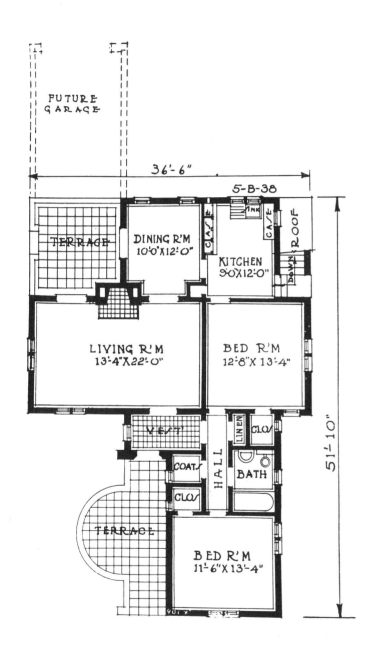

FUTURE GARAGE

36'-6"

5-B-38

TERRACE

DINING R'M
10'-0"X12'-0"

KITCHEN
9'-0"X12'-0"

DOWN ROOF

CASE CASE

LIVING R'M
13'-4"X22'-0"

BED R'M
12'-8"X13'-4"

51'-10"

VEST

HALL

LINEN CLO.

COATS

BATH

CLO.

TERRACE

BED R'M
11'-6"X13'-4"

Floor plan and sketch of living room, "Spanish Bungalow."

115

The Georgian Colonial Revival Style

What the early settlers achieved in architectural simplicity, their descendants "improved" upon. As with many other revivals, that of the Colonial was an attempt to recapture a style of the past which had nostalgic appeal and symbolic importance. Colonial Revival is Georgian Colonial writ large in columned porticoes, Palladian and bow-front windows, massive brick chimneys, and elaborate exterior and interior millwork. Following the Centennial, interest in replicating the Colonial heritage slowly grew in strength. During the 1880s and '90s some of the most fashionable architects in New York and Boston carefully reproduced Georgian features in homes, club houses, and churches. By the 1920s, when Williamsburg was first hatched, the Colonial Revival became as middle class as Dick and Jane's red brick house. In the post-World War II period, it invaded the countryside in Howard Johnson subdivision form, and there it has stayed—America's true architectural sweetheart.

Now over 100 years old, Colonial Revival has in itself become antique. It is hard, however, to envision historic status being granted at some future time to a majority of the 1970s homes being built in the Neo-Colonial tradition. The Colonial Revival ran out of steam by the 1920s in terms of stylistic integrity and handling of materials. Some architectural historians would probably claim that only the very first buildings in this style by Arthur Little, McKim, Mead and White, and Charles A. Platt qualify for serous study. Our concern in *Old House Plans*, however, is not with the stylistically pure but with the vernacular. Yet a number of experts look back with some admiration on the later practitioners of the style. As Marcus Whiffen notes in *American Architecture Since 1780*, "the Neo-Adamesque façades that went up in such numbers along the streets of New York and other cities in the 1920s constitute the last consistent street architecture that America has had."

Whiffen points out that architects working in this style depended on two traditions for their inspiration—the Georgian Colonial and the Federal. The Neo-Federal or Neo-Adamesque proportions and detailing, as pointed out elsewhere in this book, relate strongly to the Neo-Colonial. As the Federal was an appropriate style for urban town houses in the early nineteenth century, so, too, was it adopted and adapted in Eastern cities during the early years of the twentieth century. In surburban and rural areas, Georgian Colonial and even earlier and more rustic versions of the domestic vernacular were the order of the day. As is evident in

the first 1920s house plan presented, the dimensions of the average house are considerably greater than those found in either most middle eighteenth-century or mid-twentieth-century Colonials. Each floor shown measures 1,390 square feet; the principal rooms on the first floor, each 15 x 19 feet, are more than ample for furnishing in period furniture and for entertaining in a graceful manner. Provision has been made for the work and housing of servants. This was the 1920s, a time when the prospering Arrow-collared executive or professional had a great deal more discretionary income; a live-in servant was not at all the sole privilege of the rich. In keeping with the tenor of the times, each of the end walls of the house is flanked with a "piazza," a most un-eighteenth-century feature. It is such additions as these, intermixed with a Colonial profile and detailing, which define the style of the time.

The basic form of a center-hall Colonial is followed quite closely. The arched portico and entryway with fan- and sidelights, the cornice dentils, the shutters, the brick chimneys at each end, and dormer windows further define the Georgian Colonial. The structure itself is of brick laid in Flemish bond; the roof is of "particolored" rough slate. The sash windows with six over six lights are decidedly modern, although they are set in a traditional wood surround with wood sills. At least one interior feature of the house would have pleased any Colonial gentleman and his lady or today's energy-conscious home owner. At least six rooms are supplied with fireplaces. Their use in the '20s, however, was primarily decorative. A modern resident of such a dwelling might find it necessary to install a bathroom or "powder room" on the first floor of the house. There is ample room for such an improvement. In fact, in order to keep fuel bills under control, the attic rooms, at least, might be closed off in the winter months.

All the wood trim in the house, exterior and interior, was to be painted white. The dining room was wood-paneled and painted in a mat glaze oil. The walls of the formal front hall and "parlor" (the term persisted into the twentieth century) were covered in the same paper. Mouldings were minimal and included in most of the rooms only a hardwood shoe. Floors in the dining room, parlor, and first and second-floor halls were of hardwood and most probably were covered with oriental or braided rugs. Other rooms had softwood flooring which was carpeted. The kitchen floor was finished in linoleum; that of the bathrooms was ceramic tile, this

Proposed "Colonial" home, 1922. In the '20s a residence of this
sort was as thoroughly modern and distinguished as the pha-
eton drawn to the curb.

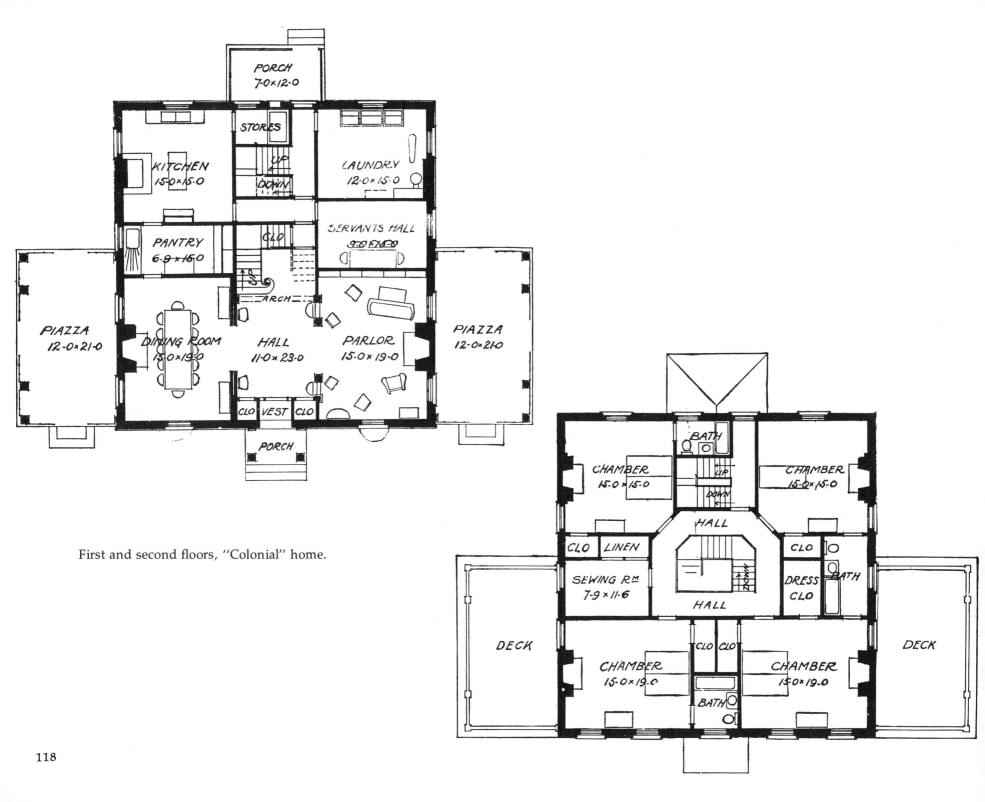

First and second floors, "Colonial" home.

covering continuing up the walls several feet. To mitigate dampness problems in the bathrooms, walls and ceilings were finished in cement and painted with enamel oil paint. All walls in the house, of course, were of lath and plaster; plasterboard had yet to come.

Details in other Colonial Georgian Revival homes included exterior clapboarding, shingling, stuccoing, and fieldstone facing. Clapboards ranged in width from about nine to three and a half inches. Roofs were often of the hip variety, and sometimes included a balustraded deck. A Palladian window was frequently centered at the second-story level in a pediment which broke the roof line. Interior detailing might include wainscoting, the use of chair rails, and elaborate fireplace wall and doorway mouldings. Some houses in suburban areas of New England and of the Middle Atlantic states were so successful in their reproduction of the Colonial that only a dating of structural materials will establish a building's true age.

The historical importance of the Colonial Georgian Revival house should not be exaggerated. In the hands of a master architect, however, a dwelling of considerable grace and strength emerged with a distinct and valid style. Denver, Colorado, has just established the first historic landmark district of such homes; others in time—if saved—will take their place on the registries of architecturally significant buildings.

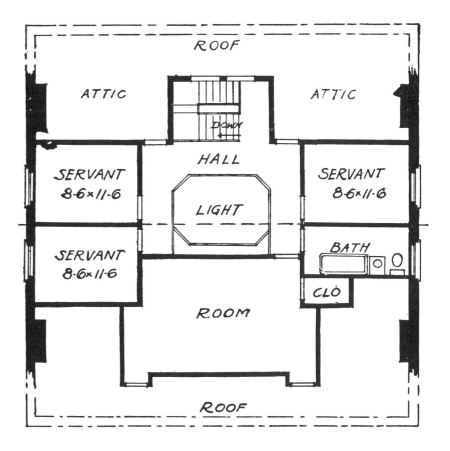

Third floor, "Colonial" home.

Proposed "Georgian Colonial" residence using narrow clapboard and featuring a Palladian window, 1922.

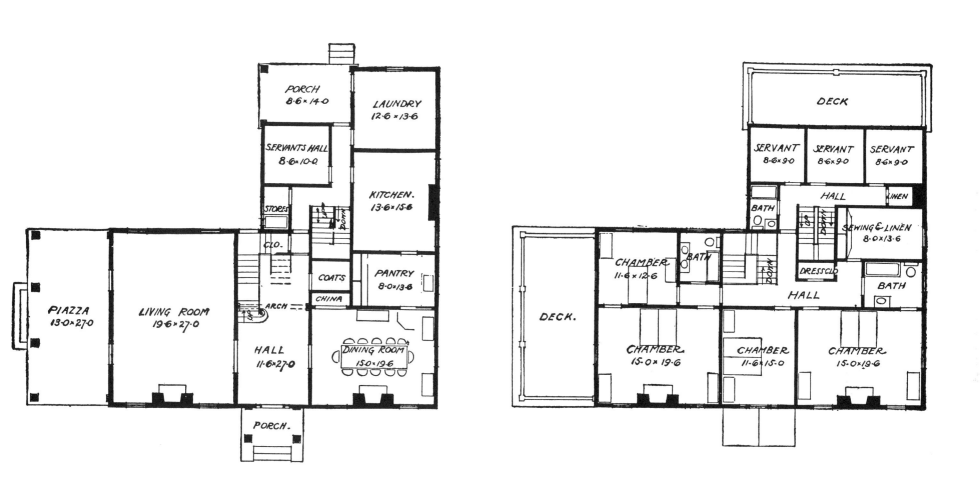

First and second floors, "Georgian Colonial" residence.

L. K. Hazard House, Elizabeth, New Jersey, A.L.C. March, architect, New York, 1892. The gambrel roof was adopted from numerous eighteenth-century models of the Dutch, Swedish, and English Colonial. The two intersecting gables are incorporated in a structure that makes use of high-style Queen Anne and Georgian Colonial architectural elements.

House at Glen Ridge, New Jersey, William A. Lambert, architect, New York, 1901. The boxy, hip-roofed Colonial has been decorated in wedding-cake manner.

"A True Colonial," 1928. By the 1920s, the "Colonial" had been stripped of most of its Queen Anne and Beaux Arts details. What had finally emerged was a simple vernacular structure that featured instead a somewhat ornate doorway and nonfunctioning shutters. This basic model would remain popular until at least the 1950s.

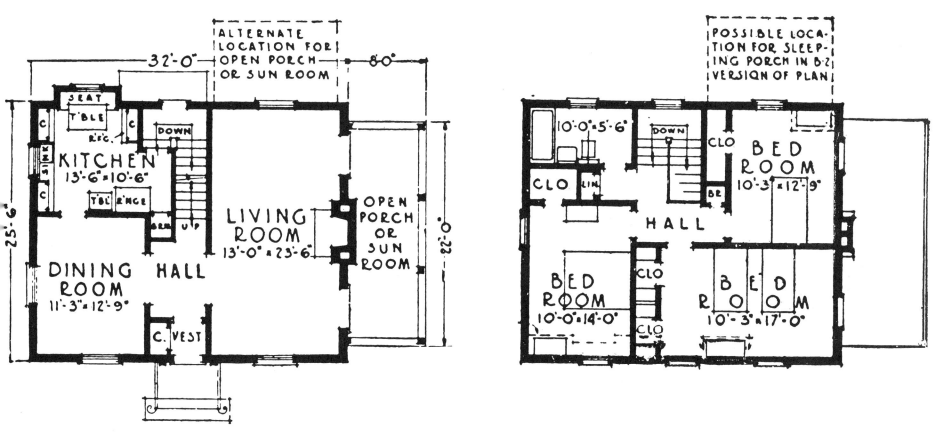

First and second floors, "A True Colonial." Note that there is no provision for an attached garage, an absolute necessity by the Age of Eisenhower.

"Colonial Brought Up-to-Date," 1928. Again, a three-bay "Colonial," but one that emphasizes a more rustic appearance with a second-floor overhang and pendants. This model, with attached garage, is still being built across America.

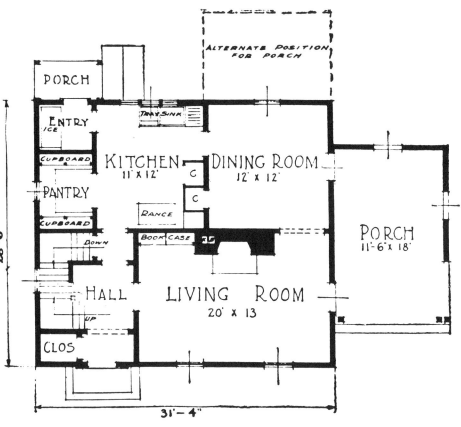

First and second floors, "Colonial Brought Up-to-Date."

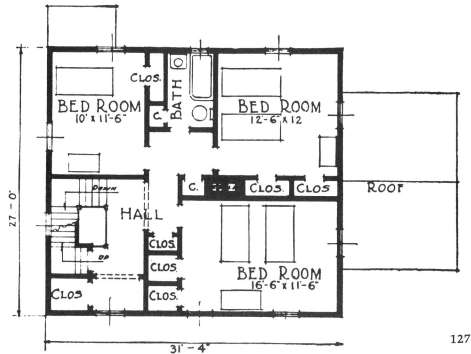